# THE GOLDEN HILLS OF CALIFORNIA

These hills are not called golden merely because gold lies hidden beneath them. The early visitors to the coastal waters of the state saw whole hillsides covered with poppies. The golden poppy, Escholtzia, has become the state flower, although few of the flatlanders have ever seen the hills in bloom.

Here, in the foothills of the Sierra, each spring brings back the wealth to the hillsides. The fields are alive with color, not only gold, but every conceivable color, all embroidered on a rich tapestry of green. The wildflowers may be humble in themselves, each no larger than a fingertip, but taken all together they have the appearance of bright brush strokes on the canvas of the countryside.

The summer brings gold, too—the gold of the dried grass undulating beneath a sky of deep blue.

With the approach of winter, the leaves of the oaks turn golden. The cottonwoods that the pioneer farmers planted as windbreaks resemble great pillars of yellow flame. Higher in the mountains, the dogwood and the quaking aspen turn the same color, as the brisk wind makes them flutter among the pines.

After the first snowfall of winter, the Sierra Nevada once again becomes the snowy range that the Spanish saw across the Central Valley when they named it. There is no more beautiful land on the face of the earth. We hope this book will help you enjoy it.

# THE GOLDEN HILLS OF CALIFORNIA

*A Descriptive Guide to the Mother Lode Counties
of the Southern Mines, including Mariposa, Tuolumne,
Calaveras, and Amador.*

Illustrated, with maps and points of interest, natural phenomena
and historical highlights.

By Allan Masri and Peter Abenheim

**Western Tanager Press**

Santa Cruz

**Western Tanager Press/Valley Publishers**
**1111 Pacific Ave.**
**Santa Cruz, California 95060**

Library of Congress Catalog Number 78-65266
ISBN 0-913548-63-4

Second Printing 1982

# Contents

# Illustrations

# Introduction

In 1848, in his State of the Union message, President James Polk casually referred to the fact that gold had been discovered in California. The discovery of gold had been rumored back East, but most of the United States considered westerners to be liars or at least braggarts, and the news had been largely ignored. But the presidential statement lit the fuse, and an explosion took place. It was called the Gold Rush, and goldseekers by the thousands headed for that part of California destined to be called the Mother Lode, the Golden Hills of this book.

That beautiful portion of California which is known as the Mother Lode country is approximately 150 miles long, and divided into the Southern Mines and the Northern Mines. The counties of Mariposa, Tuolumne, Calaveras and Amador—the area of the Southern Mines—are described in this guide book. Everywhere there is clean air, a slow pace, and the soothing sounds of the wind rustling dry grass, the music of a meadowlark or a warbler, or the rippling of a cool mountain stream. Many of the remote roads and what's to be found at the end of them—places which are laden with history—and those which are just lovely to look at are covered in these pages.

We have included as much history as seemed appropriate, so that you may know a little more about each place you visit. The stories of the Gold Rush are numerous and long, and we have condensed them greatly. We hope we have kept the most interesting parts of the best stories.

The men who swarmed all over the area in 1849 and 1850 came from many parts of the world—England, France, Italy, Spain, Chile, Panama, Mexico, Australia, and Germany. Many of them became rich. Most of them did not. Some of them went back to their homes; some stayed and pursued other endeavors.

The Mexicans who came here very early, most of them from the state of Sonora, had had experience in mining; however, others soon were able to copy their techniques and develop their own means of getting the gold from the land—from the gold pan to the rocker, from the digging of tunnels to the blasting of quartz with gunpowder, and finally to the great destroyer of the land, hydraulic mining.

Towns sprang up, some of them for a brief time, soon abandoned or torn down and moved to other diggings. Some flourished with populations as great as fourteen thousand, then in a few years dwindling to only hundreds. Roads were built, bridges were constructed, and over these food, liquor, lumber, furniture, and knickknacks were hauled, for at the end of the road there was payment in the magic metal—gold.

In the early days the roads were narrow and winding. They were muddy in the winter, dry and dusty in the summer. But the roads were busy with mule teams and oxen pulling heavily laden wagons; with stagecoaches carrying passengers and gold to and from the mines; and with people on horseback or afoot.

Then, almost as suddenly as it had begun, it was over. The readily available surface gold had been exhausted. The miners who had been moving from one new digging to another suddenly found nowhere new to go. A few large companies were doing almost all of the mining. There was no place the goldseeker could stake a new claim.

As you come around a bend on one of these lonely roads, you may hear an echo from out of the past—a muleskinner nudging his team, or perhaps the squeaking of a stagecoach wheel, or the old miner's pick striking its blows.

Modern conveniences have become commonplace in the hills today. The roads have been straightened and paved for the automobile. The gasoline station has replaced the livery stable, the train has taken the place of the stagecoach.

Today, the historic hills are being rediscovered. We have a new rush. Again, people by the thousands are coming to discover anew the treasures of the Mother Lode country— its land, its beauty, and its tranquility.

Yet there remains an overwhelming feeling of the ghostly presence of those goldseekers who came to this area, named it, searched for its treasure, lived here and died here. That presence is part of today's treasure in the Golden Hills.

# Part One:

# Highway 140—Mariposa and the Yosemite

After lying almost undisturbed by human use for thousands of years, the area which today forms Mariposa County was first entered by the Moraga Expedition in 1806. This small party was primarily concerned with finding the natives of the region and enticing them to come back with them to the missions.

*Moraga Expedition*

The Spaniards met with a good deal of resistance from the people of the Golden Hills, who withdrew into the forests at the first approach of these strange, white-skinned beings. They may have been afraid of the men, with their armor, rifles and pack animals; or they may have heard about the missions from their friends along the coast. But the Spaniards made few converts on this first voyage.

The explorers found a new land, beautiful, strange and nameless. As they were making the first maps of the region and had to have names to put on the maps, they became the first name-givers for the Golden Hills.

Joaquin Miller, who became known as the Poet of the Sierras at a much later date, explained how this naming business happened: "In California, things name themselves, or rather Nature names them, and that name is visibly written on the face of things and every man may understand who can read."

*Joaquin Miller*

Moraga and his party, having marched toward the south for a long time without finding water, prayed that they might find a river. When their prayers were answered, they called it Rio de Nuestra Senora de la Merced, the river of our lady of mercy. Today it's known simply as the Merced, one of the most beautiful streams in the world.

At some distance south of the river, they came to a place in the forest that teemed with butterflies. They called it Las Mariposas, the butterflies. Later the same name was given to the graceful lilies that abound in the spring, because they resemble creamy white and yellow butterflies that have settled on a blade of grass.

## Highway 140—The Yosemite Highway

Highway 140 is a wide, smooth highway. Its builders took out all the bumps and curves that are the trial and joy of driving in the foothills. It will take you only too quickly through the heart of the county of Butterflies and into the sacred valley of the Ahwahneechee Indians.

No other area in the Golden Hills has more ghost towns than Mariposa, many with not even a name left on the map to show where thousands of men lived, worked and played. Even the graves were only temporary affairs, rings of stones marked by a wooden cross. The thousands of Chinese workmen who came to work here didn't leave even that much. The contracts they made with the companies back home stipulated that their remains would be returned to China, and so they were, even if they had lain in the California soil for fifty years before their final voyage.

Most of the gold rush towns followed the same pattern. After gold was discovered, men came by the hundreds, perhaps even thousands. In their haste to strike it rich, they had no time to build solid structures. Their homes and stores were tents. The most substantial had a wooden floor. Then the gold ran out, and the town vanished. Sometimes no building was left which could withstand the weather and the brush fires. Other times, a stone building would be left on the site, to be taken apart gradually by treasure hunters or farmers building stone walls or a fireplace.

After the gold rush, Mariposa proved more hospitable to sheep and cattle than to people. Today fewer than 8,000 people live here. For over a century Hornitos was the only incorporated city in the county. When it was finally

*Hornitos*

disincorporated by the legislature, Mariposa County was left with none.

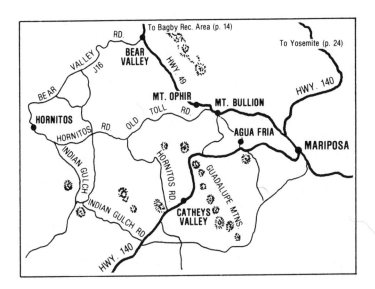

## Highway 140—Cathey's Valley to Mariposa

As you drive toward Mariposa on 140, you will pass by Cathey's Valley. This town is a relatively modern one, although the name is old. The first settler in the region was Andrew Cathey in 1854. He grew fruit and vegetables for sale to the miners. As he used Chinese laborers to clear his land and build the stone fences so characteristic of them, the place was long referred to erroneously as Cathay Valley, and natives still pronounce the name as if it had an "a" in it.

*Cathey's Valley*

Above Cathey's Valley, the road leads through the Guadalupe Mountains. The ascent of the Sierra Nevada does not consist of a single grade, but instead of a series of "steps" between level areas. This range is one of those steps.

*Guadalupe Mtns.*

From the summit, you can get a good view of the Spanish land grant known as the Rancho De Las Mariposas. Much of the early history of the county centered around this grant and its flamboyant owner, James C. Fremont, who was known as the Colonel.

*James C. Fremont*

The first historical site inside the borders of the land
*Agua Fria* grant is Agua Fria. When the original 27 counties of
California were laid out in 1850, this was made the county
seat of Mariposa County. The borders of the county were
not the same as they are today. It was an immense tract of
land, stretching from the Tuolumne River in the north to
the San Gabriel Mountains in the south, and bounded on the
east and west by the Nevada state line and the Coast
Ranges respectively.

All of the original Mariposa County was wilderness.
There were no towns, aside from a few gold mining camps,
no roads, and no inhabitants other than the natives and the
miners, between whom there was frequent hostility. The
mountains were filled with wild animals, including the
cougar and the grizzly bear; their streams were wild and
impassable during the winter, bone dry in the summer. The
great central valley, today one of the leading agricultural
regions of the world, was then poorly drained bottom land
with large, stagnant lakes.

The name Agua Fria, meaning "cold water" in Spanish,
came from the creek which flowed into the valley from the
south, where it was fed by cool springs. At that time, it was
a prosperous camp, with large deposits of surface, or
placer gold, and prospects for several quartz mines.

The first quartz mine was opened in this area by Sonoran
miners in the employ of Fremont. Early lithographs of the
valley show the land cleared, the valley filled with wood-
frame houses, and a large aqueduct which had been constructed to bring water to the claims.

By 1852 Agua Fria had lost most of its miners to richer
*Mariposa* camps. The county seat was moved to Mariposa. The town
was disappearing as rapidly as it had appeared, leaving no
record on the site to mark its existence.

The hills are now covered by chaparral. These shrubs are
characteristic of the foothills. The two most common ones
are manzanita, easily recognized by its red bark and twist-
ed branches, and ceanothus, which has large flowers in the
springtime with a distinctive, sweet aroma.

The chaparral is vulnerable to fire, and this may account
for the total disappearance of Agua Fria and some of the
other camps. The swift growth of this kind of ground cover

may also be obscuring some of the traces which would otherwise be visible. It is certainly difficult to explore any area covered with dense and sharp-pointed foliage.

Not far along the highway is Mariposa, the county seat. The prosperity of the town originally depended upon the Mariposa Mine, discovered by Fremont's scout, Kit Carson, in 1849. The Mariposa operated off and on until 1956. Today the metal most important to the county's economy is not gold, but tungsten. *Mariposa*

*Kit Carson*

With a population of about 1,500, Mariposa is the largest town in the county. It is a beautiful, peaceful town with wide streets and big old houses. It was originally built closer to the creek, but that settlement was washed away during the winter of 1850, and the sad but wiser miners decided to move their town farther up on the hillside.

The miners found out about mining the same way, the hard way. Today we can find out all about it (and its history) at the excellent modern museum in Mariposa.

Of course it all began with the pan, but that was only the beginning. Even the very first miners did not find the panning method of mining gold profitable enough. In an effort to speed up the process of washing the sand until only the heaviest particles were left at the bottom of the container, a number of inventions were tried. One of these was the long tom, which duplicated the natural process of gold deposits made in river bars. The "bars" in the long toms were pieces of wood, or riffles, which caught the heavier gold-bearing sand as water passed over them. The riffles were just large enough to prevent any gold nuggets from slipping by—although the miners generally looked over the gravel at the bottom of the tom to make sure this hadn't happened. *Gold Mining Methods*

Another development was the rocker box or cradle. These were portable and more efficient than the long toms, but they could only be very small by comparison, and thus not fast enough for the average miner. The Chinese used them extensively, however, and during the 1870s many Orientals made a living by sifting and resifting the heaps of tailings left by earlier miners.

By that time hydraulic mining had replaced the more labor-intensive forms favored by the Americans. Using this system, with a compressor, a hose and a nozzle called a monitor, a few men could wash down several times the amount of dirt that they could have processed by more primitive methods. Hydraulic mining would probably be continuing to this very day if it were not for the disastrous effect it had on the low-lying farmlands. The vast quantities of dirt washed down by the monitors clogged the streams in the valleys, causing them to overflow their banks and leave deposits of rocks and slime, called slickens, on the farmland.

Because of the slickens, hydraulic mining was outlawed in 1883. Even today its effects can be seen in many parts of the state, where hillsides remain stripped to the bedrock, and the rocks have been carved into weird shapes by the high-pressure streams of water.

Another variation of placer mining was called drift mining. Most of the drift mines were discovered in the late 1850s, at places like San Andreas and Table Mountain, where the stream beds had been covered by landslides, earthquakes, or lava flows, so that tunnels had to be dug to reach the gold-bearing gravel. The gold was then separated from the valueless sand by the usual methods.

Lode mining was completely different. In a lode mine the gold was trapped in rock, frequently quartz. In order to extract the gold, the rock had to be crushed. The Mexicans employed a simple machine called an arrastra for this purpose. It consisted of a flat, circular space which had been covered with hard, flat rocks. In the middle of this circle stood a post to which was attached a long pole. A mule or some other animal was hitched to the other end of this pole, and heavy boulders were attached to the pole by means of chains. When the mule walked around the circle, the boulders were dragged across the flat bottom of the arrastra, where ore was placed for crushing.

A similar principle was employed in the Chilean Arrastra, which consisted of two stones, a round flat one on the bottom and a round one with a conical bottom on the top. The top stone rolled around the apex of the cone to crush the ore.

The arrastras were soon replaced by stamp mills. These had heavy weights attached to the ends of long poles which

were raised and lowered like a piston engine. The Mariposa
Museum has a full-scale, operative five-stamp mill in its
courtyard. The largest mills had a hundred stamps, and
generally were built beside rivers so that they could operate by water power.

*Mariposa Museum*

There was gold in the gulches here, and there was gold in
the quartz veins extending deep under the earth, but early
developers overestimated the worth of their claims. They
expended tremendous sums of money on mining equipment—mills, timbers, pumps—only to discover that a
promising vein petered out within a few feet of the surface.

Gold mining has always been a tricky business. When a
vein disappeared, it was sometimes possible to find it again
and reap huge rewards. It was also possible to go bankrupt
trying.

The Mariposa courthouse is also worth a visit. Located
near the east end of the town on the uphill side of the
highway, the courthouse is a charming old building as
peaceful and tranquil as the rest of the town. The main part
of the courthouse was built in 1854, while the clock tower
was added in 1866. It is the oldest courthouse in California
in continuous use, and the courtroom on the second floor
still has some of the original furnishings.

*Mariposa courthouse*

In front of the courthouse stands a stone monument
composed of various minerals native to the county. On top
is a large quartz crystal of unusual size and clarity.

Other buildings dating from the early days include the
jail, the Odd Fellows Hall, and St. Joseph's Church, an
attractive white structure which was built in 1862.

*St. Joseph's Church*

One of the earliest businessmen in the county was Louis
Trabucco, whose well-constructed stores and warehouses
are still standing in Mariposa, Mt. Ophir and Bear Valley.

The *Mariposa Gazette*, first known as the *Mariposa Chron-
icle*, proclaims itself the oldest weekly newspaper in continuous publication in the state. Its founder is credited with
the phrase, "Above the fog, below the snow," when
describing his hometown. It could also apply to the rest of
the foothills, for the coastal and tule fogs seldom rise above
1,000 feet and snow seldom lingers below 4,000 feet.

*Mariposa Gazette*

**Side Trip from Mariposa: Highway 49—Mariposa to Bagby.** As you drive north along Highway 49 from Mariposa, you should be aware that all of this land once
*James C.*    belonged to a single person, James C. Fremont. The extent
*Fremont*    of his ranch is shown on the accompanying map. The unusual feature of this ranch was that it had no fixed location. It would have been impossible to fix its boundaries in 1846, since the land had not been surveyed, or even

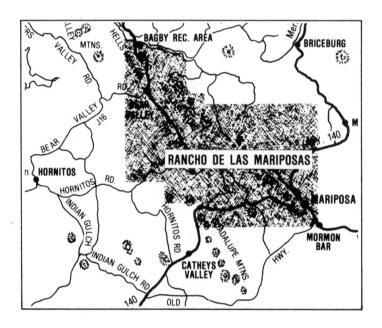

visited by its owners, the agents of the Mexican government. The deed purchased for Fremont from the Mexicans gave him ten square leagues (about 70 square miles) within certain poorly defined borders. Such a ranch was called a floating grant. These grants caused endless bitterness and made the fortunes of many early lawyers, and a few judges as well.

After gold was discovered, Fremont had the land surveyed and carefully outlined a tract for himself that included most of the gold fields, and also a site on the Merced River suitable for the construction of a mill. This gave the Rancho de las Mariposas the shape of a frying pan, and it was commonly referred to as the frying pan grant.

Fremont had more success in his ploy than the unfortunate Andres Pico in Amador County, and his personal and political enemies were quick to accuse him of skullduggery. His claim was eventually decided in the state Supreme Court, where, it was supposed, he used his political influence to obtain an unjust verdict. *Andres Pico*

Whatever the case, Fremont's land, which he had purchased with $3,000 in 1846, he eventually sold for $3 million. Unfortunately, he had incurred a large debt due to his improvements, perhaps over a million dollars. The sale of the ranch was only the beginning of the Colonel's problems with the law. The French company which had purchased the grant became upset when it operated the mines for a few months with only a fraction of the anticipated return. They accused Fremont of fraud and obtained a conviction against him in a French court, but he escaped to America, where his new-found fortune fell out from under him—but that's another story, one mired in the conflicting claims of history and fiction.

Across the road from Mariposa's modern airport you will find Mount Bullion, the site of the Princeton mine. This was one of the richest lode mines in the region, although its production of $3 million was only a fraction of that of the larger mines in the north. *Mount Bullion*

Fremont's father-in-law was Thomas Harte Benton, an influential Republican Senator. Because of Benton's support of hard currency as opposed to paper money, he earned the nickname "Old Bullion," and the town was named after him. The town of Benton Mills, on the Merced River at Ridleys Ferry, also took its name from the Senator. *Benton Mills*

**Side trip from Mount Bullion:** The old toll road between Mount Bullion and Hornitos was built in 1862.

Hornitos was a town that never would have existed at all, but for gold. The soil here is too hard for a plow, too alkaline for crops, and bone dry nine months of the year. There are many conflicting stories concerning its origins. The first settlers in the area were Mexicans, driven out of nearby Quartzburg by their white neighbors. The villain of the piece might have been Colonel Tom Thorne, a Texan *Hornitos*

*Col. Tom Thorne*

who brought his slaves and his prejudice against Mexicans to the gold fields with him.

However, luck favored the outcasts. They discovered even richer diggings near Hornitos. The fact that there was no water did not bother them, as they had mastered the art of dry panning, something the Americans never had time for.

Not long afterwards (all these things happened around 1849), Colonel Thorne and the rest of the Americans had to abandon Quartzburg, for the gold had become scarce. They all moved over to Hornitos, having decided that it was better to live with sinfulness than die in the midst of virtue.

A horno is a large Spanish-style outdoor bake oven, used primarily for baking large quantities of bread. A hornito would be a little oven, but no one knows why the town was named "Little Ovens." One theory is that the graves of the original settlers resembled ovens, since the rocky soil made grave digging difficult. Some of these graves may be seen on the hilltop above the town, though most have fallen prey to vandals.

*Miwoks*   Another possibility is that the hornitos were real ovens, constructed by the Indians. Unlike many Indians, the Miwoks cooked their food before they ate it. Their finely-woven baskets were used to boil water, which was done by dropping hot stones into it. Some food was roasted over an open fire, or a hole was dug in the ground, the food placed in it and then covered with live coals.

The Miwoks were looked down upon by the early settlers as being lazy. It was true that they did not work any more than they had to to survive, and this was scandalous to the hardworking Americans. One of their favorite foods was the grasshopper, which is plentiful in the summertime. Their method of catching and preparing the insects was a model of pre-industrial efficiency. First, they dug a hole in the ground and lined it with rocks. This would be the oven. Then they formed a wide circle around the hole and set fire to the grass. Any grasshopper that jumped through the flames would be chased back into the middle of them. Finally, when the fire burned itself out, all the grasshoppers would be in the oven, fully roasted and ready to eat, or to be ground into powder and stored for later use.

Whatever the reason for its name, sometime around the start of the gold rush there was a large town on this site called Hornitos. It was a multi-racial, multi-lingual town. The white settlers were frequently referred to as Americans, although Germans, Italians, French, and Englishmen were found among them. The Mexicans made up a large portion of the population, although they were sometimes confused with Chilenos and other Spanish-speaking people. Many of the white Southerners brought their Negro slaves with them, who were either freed or sent home for sale when California was admitted as a Free State. Then there were the Chinese, who came in great numbers and worked as miners and as laborers.

*Hornitos*

The Mexicans in Hornitos were supposed to be a wild bunch, frequenting fandango halls, saloons, and gambling casinos. The Americans were a more law-abiding breed, who preferred to build churches and lodge halls, but they must have had their dance halls, saloons and gambling casinos as well. The Chinese rarely drank, but were addicted to games of chance and (some of them) to opium.

Around the turn of the century, Hornitos had been abandoned by most of its populace and was becoming a ghost town. As it had had several thousand inhabitants at its peak, there were quite a few buildings and the place became popular with tourists. The quickest way to destroy a ghost town is for it to become popular with tourists, and today there is little left to see here.

The largest building is the brick store formerly operated by Domingo Ghirardelli. He was one of the many entrepreneurs who made fortunes with a chain of stores in the gold camps. He later became famous as the Chocolate King of San Francisco. Someone has decided his store in Hornitos makes a good garbage dump.

*Ghirardelli*

The town has a small park for the kids to play in, and a bar. The best preserved old building is a large stone store, closed up by the heavy iron shutters which are a feature of so many of the old buildings. There is also a small stone jailhouse which was used as a holding cell for prisoners until they could be taken to the county seat for trial. It has been turned into a museum by the Clampers, a fraternal lodge whose efforts sometimes seem more hysterical than

*Indian Gulch*

historical. The motto above the doorway of the jail is fractured Latin for "I believe because it is absurd."

Another approach to Hornitos is on Indian Gulch Road, which runs north from 140, west of Cathey's Valley. Indian Gulch Road leads through cattle country. The peaceful countryside gives no hint of the excitement once engendered here by the precious metal that hastened the creation of the state of California in 1848. As its name implies, the road leads to Indian Gulch, once a town but now only a valley between Santa Cruz and Indian Mountains. The ruins of an old stone store are the only reminder of the town that was.

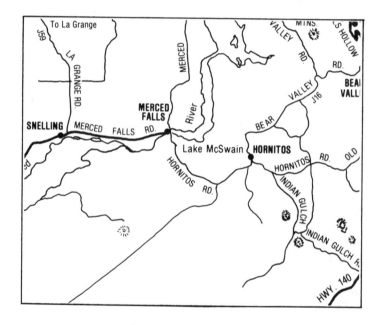

*Lake McSwain*

*Merced Falls*

**Side trip from Hornitos:** Long after the gold was gone, Hornitos remained an important crossroads between Stockton, Mariposa, and points farther south. The road west leads to the McSwain Recreation Area at the southern tip of Lake McSwain, one of the popular foothill reservoirs. Beyond that is Merced Falls, once a prosperous town where electricity was generated by water power.

This part of the Golden Hills is the best for bird watchers. Many species of hawks, kites and eagles roost in the oaks and may somtimes be seen on telephone poles by the roadside. These birds of prey subsist largely on the small rodents that thrive in the farmlands of the central valley. Efforts to restore the salmon runs in the larger streams have led to the introduction of a few bald eagles, a truly rare bird. Great blue herons have been attracted by the large reservoirs and are easily recognized by their large size, long necks and long legs.

A large number of smaller birds roost in the trees along the lower rivers, in what is known as the riparian forest. In a single morning near Snelling, 40 species and subspecies *Snelling* were sighted, and the total count of individuals was over 400. These included several varieties of sparrows, blackbirds, hummingbirds, flycatchers, towhees, and a few warblers.

The road through the lower foothills, between Snelling and La Grange, is less traveled than highway 49 between Mariposa and Coulterville. It is also less winding and faster.

**Other side trips from Hornitos:** On the Bear Valley Road, about four miles north of Hornitos, is the site of Quartzburg. Nothing remains of the town itself, which was *Quartzburg* probably moved to Hornitos for use as construction materials. The Catholic Church, St. Catherine's, is still here. It was built in 1863, not long before the town was abandoned. The church is generally closed, but services are held there on Christmas Eve by lamplight.

Continuing north on 49 from Mount Bullion, you will come to Mount Ophir. The name comes from the Bible, *Mount Ophir* where Mount Ophir is described as a land of incredible wealth. For a long time, it was thought to have been the site of the first mint in California. Fifty-dollar gold slugs, which were either hexagonal or octagonal, were supposed to have been issued here, but no records of expenditures on the mint have been discovered in Washington, and none of the old coins has come to light. If you ever come across a Mount Ophir slug, it will either be a fraud or worth a fortune.

The town of Bear Valley is a quiet place in a beautiful *Bear Valley* location. This was the place Colonel Fremont chose as the headquarters of his domain. He had been an unsuccessful

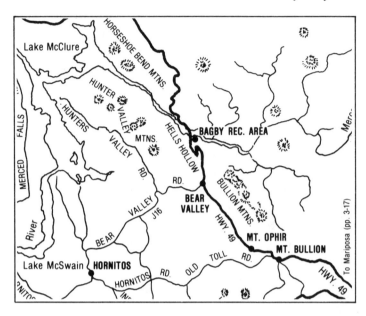

presidential candidate in 1856, so his house was humorously called the White House. It was unfortunately destroyed by fire.

*Oso House*

A more substantial early building which met the same fate was the Oso House, a hotel. Oso is Spanish for bear. This was Fremont's office, and the place where his many famous friends stayed when they visited him—men like

*Horace Greeley*

Benton and Horace Greeley. Its opulent furnishings had to be shipped around Cape Horn, and it remained intact until 1937. The present Oso House is the former Odd Fellows Hall. It has been converted into a private museum with a modest admission price of 25¢.

One of the early residents of the town was a bartender named Bigler, whose wife Margaret was the first white woman in the vicinity. Bigler was killed in a brawl, and Margaret became a single woman again, a rare status in the Golden Hills in the early days. Instead of remarrying immediately, Ms. Bigler ran a bakery and fought off admirers with a stick. Later she held a number of county offices.

Along with the Oso House, the little town has the Bon Ton Bar, a jail, a graveyard, and another store built by the ubiquitous Louis Trabucco, at the farm where he raised his produce.

**Side trip from Bear Valley:** The Bear Valley Road leads to Quartzburg and Hornitos past a number of abandoned mine sites. It also connects with the Hunters Valley Road, which leads to a recreation area on Lake McClure with camping facilities and boat ramps.

*Bear Valley Rd.*

*Lake McClure*

It should be noted that old mine sites are extremely dangerous. In addition to the obvious dangers of falling down an unlit shaft or breaking a rotten timber, the ground around the entrance to the mine is generally unstable and prone to cave-ins. Most mines have been sealed off with boulders and logs, and "No Trespassing" signs have been posted for the safety of tourists.

**Side trip from Bear Valley:** Highway 49 north of Bear Valley passes through some of the most beautiful and rugged landscapes anywhere. These cliffs rise ever more steeply from the Merced River until they become the granite monoliths of Yosemite. Early travelers reported seeing the unique formations of the valley in the distance as they crossed the Merced River at this point, but the changed position of the road now makes such sightings impossible.

*Merced River*

The site of the former resort town of Bagby was inundated by waters rising behind the Exchequer Dam in 1967. Another town has been built above the high water mark to provide access to the recreational reservoir at this point. This was the site of Benton Mills, which had 80 stamps in 1865. The mines it served, the Pine Tree and the Josephine, were located at the top of the south ridge. Rails were laid between the mines and the mill and the ore was carried down the hill by gravity, while the speed of the ore cars was regulated by a brakeman.

*Bagby*

After the decline of the mines, there was a resort hotel here, named for its owner. The Yosemite Railroad brought new prosperity to the place beginning in 1907. The railroad was an engineering feat of no small magnitude, especially since its owners were involved in a race to get to the valley first. But the age of rails was short-lived, and automobiles

*Yosemite R.R.*

were permitted to enter the valley in 1916. The railroad continued its service to the valley until 1937, when rains washed out sections of the track between Bagby and the valley. All service on the road was discontinued in 1945.

*Hells Hollow*

The road to the south of Bagby runs through Hells Hollow, an aptly named canyon with steep walls and a covering of dense chaparral. The road to Coulterville to the north is somewhat straighter.

**Side trip from Mariposa:** Highway 49 leads to the south past the fairgrounds, where the Mariposa County Fair is held every Labor Day weekend. The county may be small, but everyone goes all-out to make the fair the biggest event of the year, for both the natives and their guests.

One mile north of the fairgrounds, the Old Yosemite Highway turns off to the west. It will take you back to Cathey's Valley, or to Yaqui Gulch Road, which doubles back to Mariposa.

*Mormon Bar*

Mormon Bar is the next town on Highway 49. It was one of the few places in the Golden Hills whose history pre-dated the gold rush. Its first residents were Mormons who had come to establish the state of Deseret with its capital at

*Brigham Young*

Salt Lake City. Brigham Young had seen an opportunity to acquire a huge tract of western land after the defeat of the Mexicans in the 1846–1849 war. In 1849, he applied to the U.S. Government for statehood, with the boundaries of the state to be determined by such far-flung settlements as Mormon Island in El Dorado County, Mormon Creek in Tuolumne County, and here at Mormon Bar. When statehood was denied, the Mormons returned to Salt Lake City, ignoring the temptation of the gold fields in accordance with the demands of their faith.

The Chinese were especially numerous at Mormon Bar. Fremont charged a flat fee of $4 per month to each miner on his estate, but the Chinese were willing to pay, since in return they received protection from claim jumpers and a reasonable assurance of their personal security. The early stores of the Chinese were built of stone for the simple reason that their owners were under constant threat of harrassment or even death from the Americans and the Mexicans. Some of their stores at Hornitos had secret

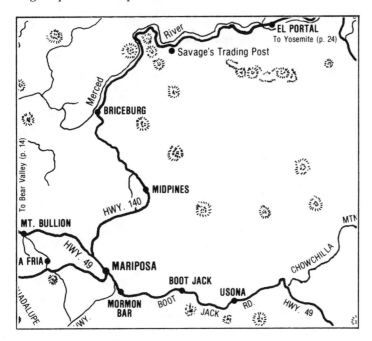

passages to allow their owners to escape their persecutors.

The Dexter Museum is another attraction of Mormon Bar. This building once housed the *Gazette* offices.

Farther down Highway 49 are the gold rush towns of Boot Jack and Usona. Located outside the boundaries of the grant, these locations were favored by the Americans who had opposed Fremont's claims in the courts and refused to pay his fee. Not far beyond Usona is the Chowchilla Mountain Road, an old route to the Mariposa Grove of Big Trees and Yosemite National Park. It is a scenic route still favored by the local residents.

*Dexter Museum*

*Boot Jack*

*Usona*

*Chowchilla Mountain Road*

## Highway 140—Mariposa to Yosemite Valley

After Mariposa, Highway 140 rises slowly to the Yosemite Valley, past increasingly taller trees and more and more impressive vistas. The towns along this road are mostly recent, although the route is of historic interest. The highway joins the Merced River at Briceburg, after which occasional glimpses may be had of the domes and spires of Yosemite.

*Briceburg*

*Miwoks*

These same views were seen by the early traders and hunters, who wondered about them, but who were never permitted to enter the valley by its Miwok residents. The Miwoks were not a united tribe, but merely a collection of small bands who spoke the same language. The name Miwok merely means "people" in the Miwok language. Therefore it is not surprising that the Miwoks who lived in the Yosemite Valley, who called the valley Ahwahnee and themselves the Ahwahneechee, could be hostile to the other Miwok tribes in the area.

*Ahwahneechee*

The Ahwahneechee hated the whites much more than they disliked their fellow Miwoks. They excluded the early settlers from their valley and tried to incite the other Indians to join them in their resistance to the white invasion.

*James Savage*

The first white man to enter the Yosemite Valley was James Savage. He was one of the most colorful of the early residents of the area, and one of the few who got along well with the Indians. After the end of the Mexican War, in which he served, Savage wandered into the Golden Hills. He learned the native language and began trading with the Indians. To cement his relationships with the numerous small bands of Miwoks, Savage took many Indian wives. Estimates range from five up to 33.

*Big Oak Flat*

In 1848, Savage was known to be at Jamestown, where he had already established a trading post. Later that same year, his Indian friends were digging up gold near Big Oak Flat, where he had a trading post. The town was known as Savage's Diggin's, but the Indians were soon run out by white miners. Following a dispute over a robbery in which a white man was killed, the Americans organized a posse and chased the wrongdoers into the hills. Coming upon a camp occupied by old men, women and children, the whites began a wholesale slaughter.

*Groveland*

It should be realized that at that time in California, a white man was seldom convicted of murder, and even less frequently punished for one. The reaction of the Americans not only exceeded any justification, it also appears to have been merely a pretext to drive the Indians from the rich diggings around Big Oak Flat and Groveland. As such, it was successful, for Savage took the Indians and his trading activities farther south and opened a store on the Fresno River and one on the Merced.

The Indians were just as capable of finding gold as the other miners, although they had not known of its existence before the arrival of the white men. They traded the yellow sand to Savage and others for clothing and blankets and whatever else caught their fancy. It did not take the Miwoks long to abandon their ancient modes of life and adopt the American's clothing, houses and food. The American policy was to set aside reservations for them and to buy them off with food and clothing. On the whole this was a wise policy, since it was much easier and cheaper than trying to fight them. In the meantime, Americans who were dissatisfied with their government's policies carried out their own program of murder and dispossession.

One of the favorite tactics of the miners was to get an Indian drunk and then arrest him for drunkenness. The timing on this legal ploy was essential, for the harvest of the whites coincided with that of the Indians. As punishment, the Indians were forced to work on the white men's farms. By the time they were released, the time for their own harvest had passed and there was little choice for them except to starve to death quietly.

To further worsen the position of the Miwoks, gold was discovered on many of the tracts given to them as reservations, while others were located on good farmland, a rare commodity at the time. The miners aggravated the situation by damning up the rivers and creeks, thus preventing the salmon from coming upriver to spawn.

Finally, the rest of the Miwoks were ready to join their brothers, the Ahwahneechee, in an uprising against the invaders. One of their preliminary moves was to attack and burn the trading post operated by Savage on the Merced River. Savage was outraged, but he was also concerned with the safety of the Indians. In an effort to convince them of the folly of warfare against the whites, he took one of their chiefs to San Francisco to show him how numerous the invaders were.

What followed must have been one of the grandest sprees in the history of the world. Savage brought a fortune in gold to San Francisco with him and he spent it all. San

Francisco was a young, lawless town, whose population
consisted of miners, would-be miners, and those whose
business it was to relieve miners of their gold. Every kind
of vice was for sale openly.

At some time during the trip, Savage must have struck
his companion in anger. Although he probably forgot about
it, the chief did not. When they returned, Savage called a
council of the Indians. He told them that the whites in the
city were more numerous than ants and he warned that
they would come to the hills to avenge any wrong done
their brothers, the miners. Then he called upon the chief
who had accompanied him to verify his statements. The
chief, however, had reached his own conclusions. He
agreed with Savage about the numbers of white men in the
city, but he did not believe they would aid the miners. They
only wanted the miners' gold, he observed. When they had
taken the gold, they drove the miners out of town with
kicks and blows, just as Savage had done to him. He did not
think it reasonable that such people should come to the aid
of the whites in Mariposa, and he called on his people to
rise up against the miners.

One of the first places attacked in the ensuing Indian
War was Savage's other post on the Fresno River, where he
was later buried. Savage himself joined the other miners in

*Mariposa Brigade*       forming the Mariposa Brigade under the leadership of
General McDougal. The war was brief and resulted in the
total rout of the Indians, who were under the leadership of

*Chief Tenaya*       Chief Tenaya. Its importance in history was that it permitted the first white man to enter the Yosemite Valley
and thus revealed the wonders of the valley to the outside
world.

Savage, who had been commissioned a Major, entered
the valley at the head of his troops on March 25, 1851. They
met with no resistance. The Miwoks evidently realized the
error of their strategy and hoped to gain more by concilia-
tion. After the war, the Ahwahneechee were permitted to
stay in the valley, but they were no longer permitted to
exclude whites. About a year later, when a party of
prospectors was driven out of the valley and two of its
members killed, the miners organized a posse to drive the

Indians out of the valley. The Indians had to flee over the mountains and stay there until things settled down.

The Indians continued to live in the valley, alongside the white settlers, but their days were numbered. The younger generation accepted the ways of the white men and the older generation died of diseases, drunkenness, and old age.

An historic marker has been set up on the site of Savage's trading post on the Merced River, not far from Highway 140 at the mouth of the South Fork. Although his business was restored after the end of the hostilities, Savage was the object of hatred and envy to many of his fellow Americans. While momentarily disarmed in a scuffle, he was killed by one of his business rivals. *Savage's Trading Post*

It did not take long for a calmer, more civilized element to prevail in the Golden Hills. James M. Hutchings was one of the influences in the direction of law and morality. In the early 1850s he began his publishing career with a broadsheet called *The Miner's Ten Commandments*. This was a list of common-sense rules, accompanied by appropriate illustrations. The miners were advised to hold only one claim, to abstain from gambling and liquor, and to remember the folks back home. *The Miner's Ten Commandments* was immensely popular, selling thousands of copies, and starting its author and publisher on a long career as a publicist. The illustrations in his work may have been more important than the text. It is certain that many of the men who bought his broadside could not read, but they could all understand the pictures. *James M. Hutchings*

*The Miner's Ten Commandments*

In 1855, while he was the publisher of *Hutchings' California Magazine*, Hutchings made his first visit to Yosemite Valley. He immediately began a series of articles, pamphlets and books bringing the wonders of the Sierra Nevada to the attention of an unbelieving public.

In 1864, President Abraham Lincoln signed a bill ceding the Yosemite Valley and the Mariposa Grove of Big Trees to the State of California for development as a park. Galen Clark was named the park's first guardian. He made his headquarters at Wawona near the grove of Sequoias that he had discovered. Unlike Hutchings, who publicized everything including himself, Clark was a quiet, self-effacing *Galen Clark*

*Wawona*

woodsman. When one of the trees was named after him, he took down the sign. A mountain peak also received his name, but he said he couldn't do anything about that.

*John Muir* Another man with an important role to play in the development of Yosemite National Park was John Muir. Although a native of Scotland, Muir was as American as anyone else when he stepped off the boat in San Francisco, having spent his childhood and young adulthood in Madison and Indianapolis. He reportedly didn't care much for the city by the bay. His first action was to stop a passerby and ask him how to get out of town.

"Where do you want to go?" came the response.

"Anywhere that's wild," asserted Muir, whereupon the San Franciscan directed him to the Oakland ferry.

Despite his vague reply, Muir had a goal already, the Yosemite Valley. He had probably read some of Hutchings' stirring accounts of its wonders and decided to see the place himself. He and a friend made the journey together on foot. *Bridal Veil Falls* As they caught sight of Bridal Veil Falls in the distance, his friend remarked about how distance distorted perception.

"Take that waterfall," he said to Muir. "From this distance it looks no more than 15 feet high, but I'll wager it's 50 or 60." Bridal Veil Falls is 620 feet high.

John Muir was tremendously impressed with what he saw in the valley. He decided to stay, and Hutchings gave him a job and a cabin. That year, 1868, there were 600 visitors and Hutchings was the best known guide, but Muir soon changed that. He was college educated and had many friends in academic circles. His writings on wilderness, flora and fauna, and especially geology, became popular *Joseph LeConte* among the intellectuals, and they sought him out. Joseph Le Conte, who was a professor at the University of California, *Ralph Waldo* came to see him, as did Ralph Waldo Emerson, in 1871.
*Emerson*

Hutchings may have been jealous of the younger Muir, who was becoming more popular and famous than himself, but he had other problems as well. He owned 160 acres of land in Yosemite Valley which the state government was trying to get away from him, on the grounds that there could be no private ownership of lands in the valley. Hutchings waged a long court fight before being forced to sell out.

He continued his career, publishing and writing about the Yosemite Valley and the Big Trees. His daughter, Florence, was the unofficial greeter of the stagecoaches bringing visitors to the valley. She shocked everyone by running around barefoot and smoking cigars.

Hutchings died in 1902 on the treacherous switchbacks of Big Oak Flat Road, not far from the floor of the valley. He never mentioned John Muir in any of his writings, but history played a trick on him by making Muir famous and forgetting Hutchings, who had been known as the Father of Yosemite. One of his quirks was about the spelling of the word Yosemite, which means Grizzly Bear in the dialect of the Ahwahneechee. Hutchings insisted on some other spelling, be it Yo Hamite, Yo semite, or something equally bizarre. The Indians were no help, as they hadn't taken the trouble to invent an alphabet.

John Muir married in 1880 and left the valley to live on a ranch in Martinez. He never stopped writing about the Sierra, however, or concerning himself with the preservation of the wilderness. In 1890, largely due to his experiences and his writing about them, the Federal government made the area around the valley into a National Park. The overriding reason for the park was to preserve the streams that fed the waterfalls. Muir had long since pointed out the danger from sheep grazing there, calling the sheep "four-footed locusts."

In 1892, Muir was elected president of the Sierra Club, whose purpose was to preserve and protect the wilderness areas of the mountains. Hutchings and Galen Clark were charter members, along with Frederick Olmstead, whose political influence was instrumental in the success of the club's politics.

*Sierra Club*

*Frederick Olmstead*

Muir was shocked to discover how badly the Yosemite Valley was being cared for by the state. He was successful in his attempt to get the state to hand over the care of the park to the National Park Service.

Another victory came in 1897 when the first National Forest Preserves were created by President William McKinley. Later, two presidents received guided tours of the valley from the aging Muir: Teddy Roosevelt and William Taft. Under their administrations, the Sierra Club was

successful in its campaign to save the Hetch Hetchy Valley
from becoming a reservoir, but one of Woodrow Wilson's
first acts was to sign legislation permitting the construction

*O'Shaughnessy*
*Dam*

of O'Shaughnessy Dam. Muir died in 1913, shortly after
learning the fate of the second great valley of the Sierra.

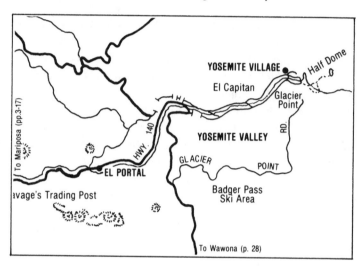

*El Portal*

Yosemite National Park begins after the highway passes
through the administrative town of El Portal. The valley
itself is about 4,000 feet above sea level. On either side of
the nearly flat valley, shear cliffs rise 3,000 feet in the air.
Falling from these cliffs are dozens of waterfalls.

*El Capitan*

El Capitan stands like a guardian at the entrance to the
valley. Its top is 3,500 feet above the valley floor, and its
walls are nearly vertical. It is the largest single block of
granite in the world. El Cap is very popular with rock
climbers, a hardy breed—some would say foolhardy. The
ascent takes the better part of three days. During the night,
the climbers attach themselves to the cliffs by means of
pitons wedged into cracks in the rock.

*Bridal Veil Falls*

Across the valley from El Capitan is Bridal Veil Falls.
When caught by updrafts, the fall flutters in the wind like
a white veil. Like the other falls, this one is most impressive

*Ribbon Falls*

in the springtime, when the snow is melting. Ribbon Falls,
falling down the side of El Capitan, has the largest single
drop of any waterfall in the park, 1,610 feet, but its creek is
completely dry in the summer.

Half Dome at dusk.

The total drop of Yosemite Falls is 2,425 feet, making it the highest fall in the United States. When at its greatest flow, in the early spring, there is no more impressive sight anywhere than the white water spreading out over the rocks like a giant fan. The Upper Falls is 1,430 feet, followed by a series of smaller falls before the water tumbles into a pool on the floor of the valley at Lower Falls (320 feet).

Another distinctive feature of the valley is Half Dome, located at the far end of the valley, and looking as though a giant knife had sliced part of it away. According to Muir's theories, this was done by the action of a giant glacier, or rather several, which descended from the vicinity of Mt. Lyell. At the time, this was a controversial theory in scientific circles. Louis Agassiz was the proponent of the Ice Ages, as he called them, while others, including Charles Darwin, believed that such formations were caused by catastrophes such as earthquakes.

Half Dome was the first rock which had to be climbed by means of bolts driven into the rock. Early climbers had been content to reach a point 100 feet below the summit, but after the first effort was made, the bolts were left in the rock so that others could enjoy the incomparable view from the summit.

*Yosemite Falls*

*Half Dome*

*Mt. Lyell*

Another favorite attraction of the early visitors was Mirror Lake. The lake is still there, but its reflective qualities were a result of its shallow waters, which are now being silted in and covered with reeds. This part of the park is off-limits to cars.

Golden mantled ground squirrel.

The park rangers and naturalists provide numerous interesting displays and lectures about the history, wildlife and geology of the park. One of the larger exhibits is a typical Miwok Village, such as the Indians used before white men came to the valley. The Miwoks inhabited the entire area of the Golden Hills from the Fresno to the Cosumnes River. A related group, the Coast Miwoks, lived in Marin County.

Their staple food was meal prepared from acorns. In some locations, the acorn festivals of the early inhabitants have been revived by the present-day Miwoks, who live on small reservations called Rancherias.

The Miwoks did not plant any crops (with the possible exception of tobacco) but they were not entirely subject to the caprices of nature, either. They cleared the forest of dry leaves and thickets to prevent the outbreak of serious fires. They also burned down the pine trees in the vicinity of the large, spreading oaks from which they obtained their food.

Due to the shrub-clearing efforts of the Miwoks, the Yosemite had quite a different aspect from its present one when it was first discovered. The vistas were clear and uncluttered by pine and cedar trees. The whole valley consisted of oak woodlands and meadows.

Although there was a certain amount of migration among these people, they generally congregated into larger groups for the major festivals. The usual tribal unit was small, no more than a few families, and they would spend the year traveling between a few established bases, depending on the season.

Their homes were simple affairs, consisting of willow frames covered with cedar or pine bark. These could be built in a few hours. The center of tribal life was the roundhouse, or dance house, where councils were held and religious rites performed. Another feature of their lives was a sweathouse, where the men would gather to take sweat baths, afterwards cooling off in a nearby stream. Besides keeping them clean, the baths were used before a hunt to remove the scent of the hunter's body.

In recent years the popularity of the valley has become a problem. The roads are crowded with cars, the trails are overflowing with tourists, parking places are hard to find and there are long waits in the cafeterias and dining rooms. As a response to this problem, part of the valley was made off-limits to cars, but this only aggravated the problems of parking and overcrowding in the rest of the valley. Soon cars may be banned entirely, but until that time those seeking the sort of wilderness experience that John Muir had in mind when he wrote about the wonders of the Yosemite Valley had better go somewhere else.

There are trails leading from the valley floor which you may take if you wish to avoid most of the crowds. One leads to the top of Yosemite Falls, and another leads to Glacier Point. Other trails continue alongside the Merced River to Vernal Falls, Nevada Falls, and the High Sierra beyond. Careful planning must be made for any sort of wilderness expedition.

Another approach to the convenient and relaxed enjoyment of Yosemite Valley is to stay at the Ahwahnee Hotel. This magnificent old building still retains much of its

Climber's view of Yosemite Valley.

nineteenth century charm, with high, broadbeamed ceilings
and hallways carpeted with oriental rugs. Dinner in the
dining room may be enjoyed without all the fuss of earlier
times, but it is still the only dining room in the Golden Hills
which requires men to wear ties and women to wear
dresses. Dinner is by candlelight, and the guests are as much
a part of the decor as the candelabra.

There are many fine picnic areas for those who prefer to
bring their own food to the park.

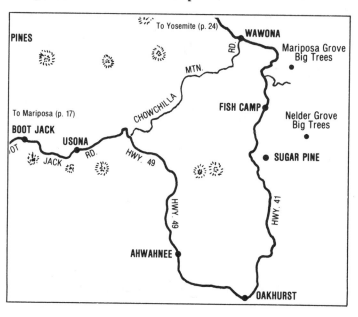

**Side trip from Yosemite Valley:** The road to the south
provides some of the best vistas of the valley. Instead of
following the course of the river, the road to Wawona rises
along the south wall of the valley, until it reaches Inspiration Point. This is perhaps the best way to enter the valley
for the first time, since there is no warning that the valley
even exists until you emerge from a long tunnel into the
sunlight. The experience is unforgettable.

*Wawona*

*Inspiration Point*

If you are leaving the valley, the process reverses itself:
first the view, then the long tunnel, then the uplands of the
park. The road to Glacier Point, which goes off to the east,
will take you past Badger Pass Ski Resort to Glacier Point.
It was from this prominence, high above Camp Curry, that

*Badger Pass*
*Ski Resort*

Cross country skiing.

live coals used to be dropped every night for the entertainment of the visitors. This spectacle, called the Fire Falls, was for many years a major tourist attraction. The red-hot embers of the fire fell about a thousand feet to a ledge beneath the Point.

The Mariposa Grove of Big Trees has always been the second great attraction of Yosemite National Park. There are about 30 groves of these trees in the Sierra. The larger groves are farther south, and contain thousands of trees, including young ones. Mariposa Grove is far from the largest, but is one of the best publicized.

*Mariposa Grove of Big Trees*

Giant Sequoia.

A tunnel was once cut through one of the larger trees, large enough for cars to pass through it. This tree, the Wawona Tree Tunnel, was one of the most frequently photographed places on earth. It fell during a storm, probably weakened by the hole cut through it.

*Wawona Tree Tunnel*

The Big Trees of California are among the world's largest living things. The General Sherman Tree, in Sequoia National Park, is often mentioned as the largest of its kind. Although it is only 272 feet tall (other trees have been measured at 320 feet or more), the Sherman Tree is 42 feet in diameter. By comparison, the Coast Redwoods, often credited as the world's tallest trees, are mere middleweights, rarely exceeding 15 feet in diameter. The tallest redwoods have been estimated at 360 feet.

The Wawona Hotel, another Victorian edifice, adds to the attractiveness of the grove area.

Not far to the south of the park is the Nelder Grove of Big Trees. Near it is Sugar Pine, an old logging camp, which has an excursion railway. Once outside the park, the Wawona Road becomes Highway 41, leading to Oakhurst and Fresno. The area to the east and south of the highway contains some of the most rugged and scenic terrain anywhere in the world. Much of this area is accessible only by pack animal and on foot.

*Nelder Grove of Big Trees*

*Sugar Pine*

The John Muir Wilderness is a fitting monument to the man who loved the Sierra so much. He called these mountains the range of light, for what is ordinary daylight in the flatlands becomes tinged with mystery here. The mountain peaks act like gigantic sundials, continually shifting the sunlight from one peak to another. In the winter, the snowcapped summits can be seen up to a hundred miles away.

Above the Golden Hills, teeming with life, rise the Sierra Nevada, the snowy mountains whose tops are as desolate as the craters of the moon. Here is one of the few places left on earth where you can feel completely alone in the wilderness, take stock of yourself, and get a renewed feeling of your own importance.

Sierra Juniper.

# Part Two:

## Highway 120—Big Oak Flat Road to Tioga Pass

If you are approaching the Golden Hills on Highway 120, you will pass Knights Ferry shortly beyond Oakdale. To see the town you must turn off the main highway about a mile, but you will find the detour well worth your while. The area around the ferry was first visited by the Bidwell-Bartelson Party of emigrants in 1841. The first man to settle here, and the one who started the ferry, was William Knight, a trapper, hunter, and a captain in Fremont's command.

*Knights Ferry*

*William Knight*

When he learned that gold had been discovered, Knight set out from his home in Knights Landing (also named for him), and wasted no time setting up a ferry on the Stanislaus. The ferry was extremely lucrative in 1849. Receipts averaged about $500 a day in some places. But Knight did not last long in the ferry business—his temper was a bit too hot—for he died that same year, probably in a dispute over a fare.

Knight's partners in the affair were the Dent brothers, who managed the ferry successfully for many years. A frequent visitor in the early days was General U. S. Grant, who was married to Julia Dent. The Dents built the first bridge in 1858, but it washed away in the record floods of 1862–63. The present bridge was built later that year, has weathered more than 100 winters and shows no sign of giving up now.

The bridge is one of the few remaining covered bridges in the state. (The old bridge at O'Byrnes Ferry, ten miles away, was recently demolished to make room for the new Tulloch Reservoir.) When bridges were made of wood, they were protected against the elements by barn-like roofs. The wooden sides were helpful in the horse and buggy days because horses often shy at the sight of water.

Table Mountain in the spring.

The street at the end of the bridge is the main street of the town. The old ferry crossed the river at the end of the main street to the right. As you turn down the street to the left, you will pass the ruins of the mill first built by David Tulloch after the disastrous flood of 1862 had washed away his previous mill. He used it to grind flour and saw wood, the normal practice in the early days before specialization. After construction of the first Tulloch Dam in 1897, the mill was converted into the first hydro-electric plant in the San Joaquin Valley.

A number of other well-preserved old buildings line the streets of the town. Not only did Knights Ferry occupy a strategic position on the Stanislaus River, it was also on the Stockton-Los Angeles Road. It was the county seat briefly in the 1850s. Bypassed by the railroad and then the State Highway, Knights Ferry has become a quiet town in a rural setting.

Ten miles west of Knights Ferry is Keystone, once only a whistle stop on the Sierra Railway, but now the location of a lumbermill. This is the best turn-off for Don Pedro Reservoir, with a 13,000 acre lake and all sorts of boating activities. The lakes in the foothills are generally stocked with bass and other game fish.

*Keystone*

*Don Pedro Reservoir*

Shortly past Keystone, Table Mountain looms into view. This strange formation was caused by an ancient lava flow. A fortune in gold was discovered underneath it.

*Table Mountain*

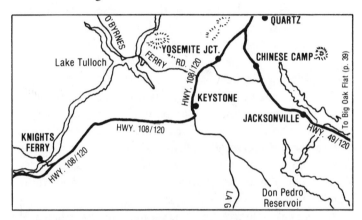

**Side trip from Highway 120:** The turn-off for Lake Tulloch's North Shore is the old O'Byrnes Ferry Road. A turn to the right from this road will take you to the site of the New Melones Dam, while straight ahead lies the town of Copperopolis. The crossing of the river at Poker Flat affords an excellent view of Table Mountain.

*Lake Tulloch*

*Poker Flat*

At Yosemite Junction, Highway 120 turns toward the south, while Highway 108 continues ahead. Highway 49 connects the two to form a triangle. It was on this stretch of Highway 49 that gold was first discovered in this region, on Woods Creek at a place called Woods Crossing. Later a mining town called Montezuma grew up on the spot, but today there is nothing there but a pile of tailings and a marker.

Yosemite Junction is the main turn-off point for travelers on the way to Yosemite Valley. Not far from the

*Yosemite Junction*

junction, along Highway 49/120, is the gold rush town of Chinese Camp. An Englishman by the name of Townsend had the idea to import laborers from China to work in the gold fields for him, and they began digging at a place called Campo Salvador. The history of the Chinese in the Golden Hills has always been obscure, largely because they did not mix with the Americans. They appear to have been indentured servants, each having signed a contract with one of the famed "six companies."

These companies were family associations in the business of providing laborers for various enterprises in California—mining, farming, railroad construction. These companies were called tongs by the Chinese, and disputes between them were called tong wars. Tong wars generally involved gambling debts or disputes over jurisdiction, as for instance when a laundry opened up too close to another one's place of business.

Every town in the Golden Hills had its Chinatown, but only one town, Chinese Camp, took its name from the orientals who lived there. Chinese Camp was the scene of one of the earliest tong wars in California, in 1856. About 1,000 men took part in the skirmish, and casualties were light, since the preferred weapon was the sword rather than the gun.

At its peak, Chinese Camp is estimated to have had 5,000 orientals in residence. The Chinese were despised by all the other miners, since they were supposed to be an inferior race and had customs that were so different from those of the rest. The greatest difference was that they were willing to work for lower wages than the Americans. They did not seem interested in taking a chance in a new location; instead, they patiently worked and reworked the tailings that other, less careful miners had already worked and abandoned. In this way, Chinese miners could still make a living, or at least supplement their incomes, by mining long after the gold rush was over. In the 1870s and 1880s, the orientals were still eking out a living in the creeks and gulches of the Golden Hills.

At the time of the building of the Transcontinental Railway by Central Pacific, Chinese laborers formed the bulk of the work force.

Today there is hardly a trace left of the tens of thousands of Chinese who lived and worked here. There are not even any graveyards, since the Chinese insisted that their remains be taken back to China after their death.

Adjoining Chinese Camp to the north was Old Chinese Camp, which came to be known as Mexican Camp because of its many hispanic residents. This, too, was a lawless town. It was at a gambling house here in 1855 that a posse from Amador County caught up with the gang of outlaws believed responsible for the Rancheria murders. There was a shoot-out that left two dead, including the leader of the posse, who had been trying to bring back the suspects alive for trial.

After the arrival of the railroad in 1897, Chinese Camp provided the fastest and least expensive means of transportation from San Francisco to the Yosemite Valley. Chinese Station was a couple of miles north of the town, and from there travelers could board stages making regular runs on the Oak Flat Road. M. M. O'Shaughnessy, the engineer who supervised the Hetch Hetchy project, made his first trip to the dam site by two-horse stagecoach in 1912. It took him four hours to reach Groveland.

Today Chinese Camp is a peaceful, forlorn little town which swelters under the hot valley sun in the summertime. It has a few old buildings, and its tree-lined, flat streets make it a pleasant place for a stroll.

Not far south of Chinese Camp, Highway 120/49 reaches the upper portion of Don Pedro Reservoir. The vista point at the north end of the bridge provides a beautiful panorama of what used to be the town of Jacksonville at the confluence of Woods Creek and the Tuolumne River.

*Don Pedro Reservoir*

*Jacksonville*

During the gold rush, the area along the creek here was teeming with miners. There was an average of one mining camp every mile, with names like Hawkins Bar, Indian Bar, Texas, Morgan, Don Pedro and Rodgers Bars. They were all located near sand bars, because gold was very apt to be deposited on the upstream side of the bar. The area's heyday was from 1850 to 1855.

The largest town was Jacksonville, where Colonel A. M. Jackson kept a store before moving on to Jackson in Amador County. That was back in 1849, but Jacksonville survived long after the other camps had vanished. It was a trading center for the quartz mines in the vicinity, as well as an agricultural community. At a farm called Smarts Gardens, many early experiments were made, including the first apple orchards and first peach trees in the Golden Hills.

Early observers report that the first peach crops in the hills were extraordinarily good but that the quality dropped off after a few years. We can safely attribute the decline to the deleterious effects of placer mining. In the end, Smarts Gardens itself was dug up by miners looking for gold.

As you look across the lake from the vista point, it is hard to imagine the sight that greeted the eyes of old-timers during the first four decades of this century. Across the creek, on the steep slope above Jacksonville, stood a 100-stamp mill and other buildings composing the external plant of the Eagle-Shawmut Mine. The mine operated until 1942 and produced $9 million in gold during the span of half a century.

*Moccasin*

*Coulterville*

At Moccasin, five miles south of Jacksonville, Highway 120 turns to the east along the route of the old Big Oak Flat Road, while Highway 49 continues south to Coulterville. Moccasin is the site of a state fish hatchery that helps keep the mountain lakes and streams stocked with trout and bass for eager anglers. In addition, Moccasin is a link in the chain of aqueducts, reservoirs and power plants that make up the Hetch Hetchy system. Here you can see the shiny metal siphon, composed of ten-foot-diameter piping, which drives the turbines at the Moccasin power plant and provides electricity to P.G. & E.'s customers in the central valley.

**Side trip from Moccasin: Highway 49 to Coulterville.** To reach the town of Coulterville, drive south from this point, continuing along Highway 49. This route is recommended for trailers and RVs because it avoids the tiresome and dangerous switchbacks of the Priest Grade.

*Penon Blanco*

Along the way lies Penon Blanco. In Spanish a penon is a large rock, like the rock of Gibraltar, while blanco means white. This ridge takes its name from the quartz veins which may be seen as white outcroppings along the crest of the ridge. These quartz veins are characteristic of the

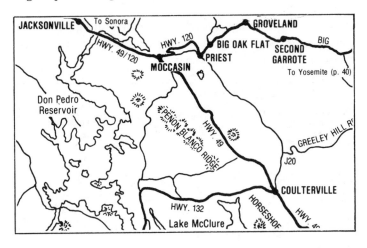

Mother Lode system. Gold is frequently discovered embedded in white quartz. The beautiful white and gold chispas (gold masses) which may be seen in various museums are a happy result of this union.

Coulterville was an early trading post and mining town. Here George Coulter kept a trading post with a big American flag next to it. Later quartz mines kept the town prosperous: the Horseshoe Bend mines were productive for a long time, as was the Mary Harrison. A very short rail line brought ore from the Harrison mine into the town, a distance of about four miles. The line was one of the candidates for the title, "the crookedest railroad in the world." The old steam engine that hauled the ore, Whistling Billy, has a permanent home in the center of town, right in front of the mining museum, which is scheduled for enlargement soon.

When the mines closed, Coulterville was left without a livelihood. For the sightseer, there is much to recommend the town. Aside from the old adobe hotel, the Jeffrey, and the restored buildings along the main street, there are a number of unrestored buildings into which the curious visitor may peer. These structures have not been restored, like the ones in Columbia, nor have they been vandalized, like those in Hornitos. As a result, some of the old furnishings remain: the old wallpapers, faded; an old safe which no one bothered to remove; the old doors with their unusual handles; the heavy steel doors and the plaster facades. These things are slowly deteriorating, but they remain just as they were when their owners abandoned them and left for greener pastures.

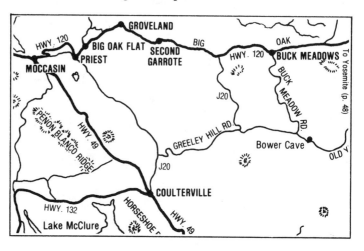

**Side trip from Coulterville:** J20, a county road, leads east from the center of town. It takes you past the old *Chinatown* Chinatown, of which two buildings remain standing. This was once a major route to the Yosemite Valley. Although it was completed at about the same time as the Big Oak Flat Road, the latter became more popular because it passed through the Tuolumne Grove of Big Trees.

Today the route is ideal for the more adventuresome traveler, especially if you have an ORV (off-the-road vehicle). The terrain is rugged, yet criss-crossed by roads in various conditions, ranging from good to dirt to hard to *Greeley Hill* find. The main road is good past Greeley Hill (named for Horace Greeley, the journalist) to Bower Cave.

*Bower Cave* The cave there, Bower Cave, is neither as impressive nor as beautiful as the two commercial caves up north, but neither is it as expensive (there is no charge). It is located on the north fork of the Merced and is a good, uncrowded spot for a picnic and a swim.

After Bower Cave, the road is slow, but not rough. There is a convenient road back to the Big Oak Flat Road about a mile east of here.

Incidentally, a Bower is a Jack in the card game of *Bret Harte* Euchre. This is helpful to know when you read Bret

Harte's famous poem, "Plain Language from Truthful James," about a Chinese card shark who played a game he didn't understand.

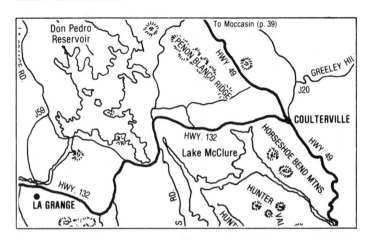

**Side trip from Coulterville:** Highway 132 will take you out of town to the west, circling around the north end of Horseshoe Bend Mountain to reach Lake McClure Recreation Area. To the north lies Don Pedro Reservoir, while Highway 132 will take you to La Grange on the old Stockton Road.

*Lake McClure*

La Grange is an interesting town to visit. Located on the Tuolumne River, it was first settled by the French, and was known as French Bar. It soon became more important for its grain than its gold. One of the first businesses was a mill operated by water power. The town takes its name from a large grain storehouse, or grange in French.

*La Grange*

Like Hornitos, La Grange was a wide-open, multi-lingual town. There were Mexicans here and the Chinese had a large settlement by the river. The largest building in the town is the Odd Fellows Hall. Louie's Place, a saloon, has a bar that was carried here from Hornitos in 1897. It is a curious fact that many ghost towns had their buildings and furnishings shipped to other towns. In this way, many fine articles were preserved from vandals and fire.

La Grange was the location of most of the dredging done in the Golden Hills. Dredging was the last method of gold mining to be developed and used. By this method, huge buckets brought gold-bearing gravel from the bottoms of the rivers. Because these dredges could process enormous quantities of ore, very poor grade ores were sufficient for the continuation of the operation. Much of the gold recovered in this manner had already been processed upstream in the quartz mills or washed down by hydraulic methods.

The two stone stores and one adobe structure in La Grange date from the 1850s. Recently a new attraction has been added by the development of a park around one of the dredges which was used until 30 years ago, then abandoned by its owners. The town could not afford to buy the dredge, but it was made the center of attraction in the park.

The dredging operations around La Grange left enormous heaps of rubble in the channel of the river, like those which may be seen around Merced Falls. This is because the dredging process turns the soil upside down, putting the smaller stones on top of the topsoil and the largest boulders on top of everything else. It is a very destructive method of mining, but its effects have been reversed around La Grange; the gravels exposed were used in the construction of the Don Pedro Dam in the 1950s.

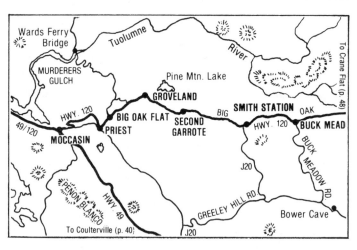

## Highway 120—Moccasin to Crane Flat

The old road climbs steeply between Moccasin and Priest. Evidently there are some hills even the most modern engineering methods can't do much about. It may be some consolation to know that the old road, originally built for

Foothill wildflowers.

wagons a century ago, was infinitely worse. It followed the route of the Old Priest Grade. The two roads meet at the top of the hill, at Priests Station.

Priests Station was a wagon stop in the mining days, and later became a resort hotel. The original hotel was destroyed by fire in 1926. Today there is a motel on the site.

*Priests Station*

Big Oak Flat is not far behind. It is a small town with a real mountainous flavor. Once again, the town owes its origin to the discovery of gold on its site. It was first worked by Jim Savage and was commonly known as Savage's Diggin's before receiving its present name from a large, wide-spreading oak.

*Big Oak Flat*

The big oak did not long survive the discovery of gold. Miners working the soil around its roots undermined the tree and it died. The numerous fires to which the town was prey have removed every trace of the tree except for a plaque and a small fragment.

The Odd Fellows Hall is the largest old building in the town. The stone store also dates from the gold rush. Both buildings had to survive the devastating fire of 1863 that almost killed the town.

People are sometimes curious about the numerous "flats" in the Golden Hills. In the case of Big Oak Flat, the confusion is redoubled by the steep incline on which the town stands. There once was a flat here, one of those beautiful mountain valleys in which the grass is green until midsummer, carpeted with multicolored wildflowers and canopied by wide-spreading oak branches. There was a flat, but it is gone, washed away by the miners' flumes in their relentless quest for gold.

*Groveland*     Groveland lies close enough to Big Oak Flat to make them seem like the same town. It was settled the year after Savage set up his store in the Flat, 1849. The soil here was literally filled with gold, and as many as 1,800 miners were working claims at the same time. Especially numerous were the French, who named the town Garotte. However, if the Mexicans were spelling it, the name would be Garrote. If the Americans were naming it, they would have called it Hangtown, for that is the English equivalent of the French and Spanish names.

By 1875, the town had no more than 100 inhabitants, many of them engaged in lode mining at the Mt. Jefferson Mine north of town, for years the main source of livelihood. It was then that the name was changed to the less ominous Groveland. The remains of the original French adobe store are enclosed inside the walls of Tiano's market. Other gold rush buildings are the Iron Door and the Groveland Hotel.

There were always many Miwoks living in the area. Long after the gold rush was finished, Miwok women panned for gold in the ruts left by wagon wheels. The first reservation in Tuolumne County was located north of the town. When the last Indian died or moved away from the land, the title reverted to the government and was either resold or given to homesteaders.

Groveland experienced another boom between 1913 and 1927 while work proceeded on the Hetch Hetchy project.
*Pine Mountain*     Since the subdivision of Pine Mountain Lake in 1969, the
*Lake*     town has been undergoing another minor renaissance. In many ways, its history is typical of the area as a whole: first, the Indians lived in harmony with nature for thousands of years. Then, miners came, shoved the Indians out or killed them, and dug gold nuggets out of the topsoil. Then, the emissaries of the burgeoning coastal metropolises came in search of pure drinking water and water for the farmlands to help feed the cities. Finally, the residents of the cities came in person, looking for relaxation and an escape from the noise and bustle of their city homes.

Old barn near Groveland.

**Side trip from Groveland:** Pine Mountain Lake subdivision adjoins Groveland on the north and east. It is an example of a suburban development which dwarfs the town to which it was attached. There are a golf course, an airport and a lake with recreational facilities. The main road through the subdivision rejoins Highway 120 at Buck Meadows.

*Buck Meadows*

**Side trip from Groveland:** Deer Flat Road meanders down Deer Creek to the Tuolumne River at Wards Ferry. This was the highest feasible spot for a ferry on the river, as there are no beaches and the canyon walls are steep. It is a lonely spot, even with the modern bridge.

*Wards Ferry*

The old trail from the ferry on the south side of the river passed through Murderers Gulch. Three tolltakers were murdered here, along with an unknown number of miners. In the early days the bandits killed their victims, both to avoid identification later and because robbery was the more serious of the two crimes. A highwayman could

*Murderers Gulch*

expect to be strung up from the nearest oak; a murderer
would be acquitted in any courtroom. Due to the steep
slope of the canyon, Murderers Gulch seldom emerges from
the shade.

The bridge is high and graceful. Thousands of swallows
make their nests of caked mud in its steel trusses. The
remains of an old cabin cling precariously to the cliff. The
cabin was probably used by the tolltakers. It is difficult to
imagine what else could make someone want to live in this
desolate place.

The road continues to Tuolumne and Sonora on the other
side of the river.

*Second Garrote*

After leaving Groveland, Highway 120 passes through
the site of Second Garrote. A story told about its name
relates that a traveler on the Yosemite stage inquired what
the name of the place might be. When he was told, he
looked around and noted the similarity of the place to
Groveland. "The hell you say!" he exclaimed. "I say this is
Second Garrote!" and so it remained.

Like so many of the old stories, this one has more
humorous than historical value.

When the Big Oak Flat Road was built in 1876, the
operators of the stage line wanted to invent a reason to
make a stop in Second Garrote. They selected a tree of
sufficient size and christened it "Hangman's Tree." While
it is not impossible that men were hanged from the branches of some of the older oaks still living, it is unlikely that
vigilante groups would designate one tree as the objective
of all their necktie parties. In such cases, the tree employed
was generally the nearest one.

*Bret Harte Cabin*

Another tourist attraction of Second Garrote was the
Bret Harte Cabin. This building had something in common
with the Mark Twain Cabin in Tuttletown: the man whose
name it bore never even slept there, much less lived there.

The Bret Harte Cabin at Second Garrote was once the
residence of two friends, Chamberlain and Chaffee. These
two miners never married. They were so devoted to one
another that one soon died of grief after the other had
passed away. It was only in this devotion (not uncommon
among the Argonauts) that the two resembled the two title
characters in Harte's famous story, "Tennessee's Partner."

Bret Harte never met the two miners. In fact, we may wonder how much of Harte's work, despite its realism and detail, was based on actual persons or real locations. Harte set his stories in places called Roaring Camp, Poker Flat, and Sandy Bar, just as modern authors have invented the cities of Zenith and Metropolis.

Beyond Second Garrote, the Big Oak Flat Road leaves civilization behind and sets out across some pretty rugged territory. This road was long an important route to Yosemite, but it was used even before the valley was discovered. Miners used it to haul supplies, lumbermen used it to bring lumber down from the hills, hunters used it in their search for game, and the water companies used it to build and service their flumes.

At Smith Station, a road to the right leads to Coulterville and Bower Cave. There are several campsites in this part of the Stanislaus National Forest not far from the highway.

*Smith Station*

Those who have not traveled on the Big Oak Flat Road recently would not recognize it, so great have been the changes made by Caltrans in the interest of faster, smoother travel.

The view of the Tuolumne River Valley and Jawbone Ridge from the spot known as Rim of the World has not changed, however. Not far past this point, the road has bypassed the old South Fork Bridge, but a short detour will take you there. Below the old bridge is Rainbow Pool and Rainbow Falls, a pleasant place for a picnic and swim on a hot summer day.

*Rainbow Falls*

**Side trip from Highway 120:** Hetch Hetchy lies about twenty miles from the main road. One way to reach it is to take the turn-off to the left about a mile and a half past the Rim of the World. Another road inside the boundary of Yosemite National Park also goes there.

*Rim of the World*

The massive granite formations of the Hetch Hetchy Valley are found nowhere else on earth—except Yosemite Valley. The resemblance in some respects is uncanny. The entrance to Hetch Hetchy is guarded by a smaller version of El Capitan, while on the right side is Kolana Rock, which is similar to Sentinel Dome. Wapama Falls, like

*Hetch Hetchy Valley*

*Wapama Falls*

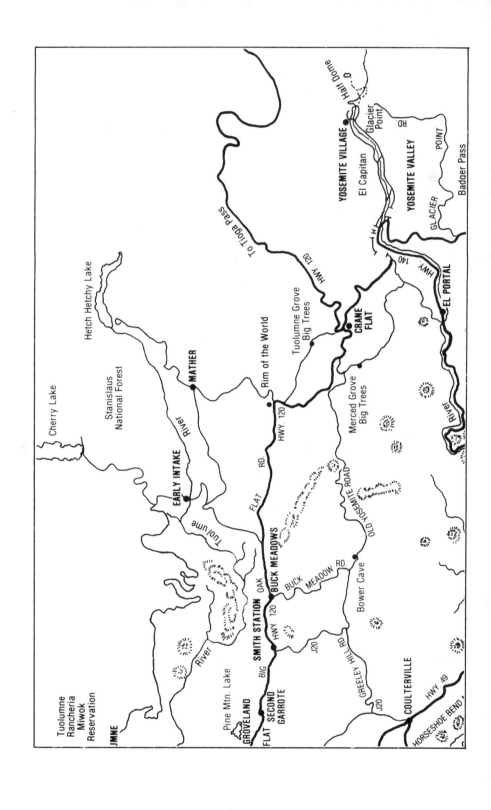

Yosemite Falls, has two major cataracts and a considerably reduced flow in the dry season.

Hetch Hetchy is much smaller, only six square miles compared with Yosemite's 30. And, of course, this valley is filled with water.

It has been asserted with some reason that if this valley had existed somewhere else, say in New Zealand or Switzerland, people would come from all over the world to admire it. But, since it is so close to Yosemite Valley, its value as a tourist attraction was virtually destroyed by filling it with water. Initially it was argued that this would only make the place more accessible and more attractive to tourists, but it has not happened that way. Very few of the millions of annual visitors to Yosemite National Park ever venture into this relatively wild region.

The alteration of Hetch Hetchy has not been all for the worse. Unlike its neighbor to the south, this valley has no problems with crowds, no air pollution, and no high-priced specialty shops. The stark silhouettes of the rocks are outlined in the deep blue waters of a mountain lake.

The dam itself is remarkable as an engineering feat. Construction was begun in 1913 after a long and bitter struggle. Construction was supervised by M. M. O'Shaughnessy, city engineer of San Francisco. It was the first project of its kind in the Golden Hills, although others soon followed. The valley was a perfect location for a reservoir for drinking water. Its isolation from civilization and animal pastures helps assure its purity. Its depth retards the growth of algae and impedes evaporation, which in turn prevents the water from becoming salty or alkaline.

Even before the dam was built, a boulder in the creek bed caused the lower third of the valley to flood in the springtime. This made Hetch Hetchy a haven for the dreaded snow mosquitoes. These little beasts may have been responsible for the destruction of the valley, as the proponents claimed that Hetch Hetchy was a mosquito-ridden bog, unfit for human habitation. Instead of drilling a short drainage tunnel to alleviate this unfortunate situation, they proposed to build a multi-million dollar dam. Such is the logic of progress.

Many Bay Area cities, including San Francisco, Berkeley,

and San Jose, have recreation camps in the general vicinity. Cherry Lake, sometimes called Lake Lloyd, can be reached by taking a turn-off at Early Intake, a power house in the Hetch Hetchy system. Cherry Lake is large, remote, and suitable for any imaginable outdoor activity.

Highway 120 enters Yosemite National Park at the Carlon Entrance Station. There is a $3 charge for passing through the park, with other fees for various lengths of stay and kinds of use. Shortly beyond the entrance, the road passes between two groves of Big Trees, the Tuolumne Grove and the Merced Grove. Neither is very large, but the groves are convenient for those who haven't time to visit larger or more remote ones.

These may have been the first Big Trees seen by the white explorers. Joe Walker's expedition of 1837 passed near them, as it passed near Yosemite Valley, but there has been a long-standing dispute as to whether Walker and his men actually saw either the trees or the valley. Since neither grove is visible from the Big Oak Flat Road, we can observe that the Indian guides of the Expedition could have prevented the Americans from seeing anything they were not supposed to, or at least from examining it too closely. The same may be said of the valley, which gives no evidence of its existence only a mile north of the rim.

Instead of descending into Yosemite Valley, Highway 120 leaves the route of the old Big Oak Flat Road at Crane Flat. The highway then proceeds across the Yosemite *Tioga Pass* watershed, through dense forests, to Tioga Pass, at 9,941 feet the highest crossing of the Sierra open to automobile traffic. Among the attractions along the way are the Grand Canyon of the Tuolumne, a long and deep defile to the *Lake Tenaya* north of the road; Lake Tenaya, named for the war chief of the Ahwahneechee during the Mariposa Indian War (this was a favorite spot of John Muir when he was a guide); and *Tuolumne* Tuolumne Meadows, a beautiful alpine meadow. The road is *Meadows* closed during the winter.

Far to the south of the road, at the eastern edge of the *Mt. Lyell* park, stands Mt. Lyell, a 13,000-foot peak. Early geologists theorized that the glacier which still persists on the slopes of this peak is the remnant of the gigantic glaciers that sculpted the Yosemite and Hetch Hetchy Valleys.

# Part Three:

# Highway 108—Sonora-Mono Highway - Tuolumne County

Tuolumne County is the largest of the four counties in the Golden Hills, but it was once even larger. The original county extended east almost to the Nevada border and west to the Coast Ranges. The present borders are the result of the formation of Stanislaus County to the west and Alpine County on the crest of the Sierra.

Visitors from the metropolitan areas of the state are sometimes mystified by the importance of county boundaries in the hills. The reasons for that emphasis are many. The towns in the hills are too small to offer many of the services which city dwellers take for granted. Thus, the Sheriff's office is the major police force. Since there are no municipalities to speak of, there are no municipal courts, only county courts. Sonora, the county seat of Tuolumne County, is the largest town in the region, with perhaps 10,000 people living in or near the city.

*Sonora*

Tuolumne takes its name from a Miwok word meaning either "those who live in stone houses" or "those who live in caves." Like practically every other word of Indian derivation, this one raises more questions than it answers. There is no record of native people living in either caves or stone houses. However, there are a large number of caves near the Stanislaus River, and the original "cave dwellers" may merely have fled to the caves to avoid contact with the Spaniards.

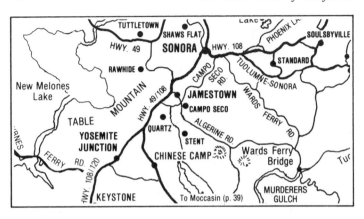

Highway 108 leaves the route of the Big Oak Flat
Road (Highway 120) at Yosemite Junction. This is very
near Woods Creek and the small mining town of James-
*Jamestown*     town. Jamestown was founded in 1848 by Colonel George
James. At first it was known as American Camp, but later
was named after its founder and leading citizen, who had
been a San Francisco lawyer before coming to the gold
fields.

In a place where towns as well as people have nicknames,
it was inevitable that Jamestown would become Jimtown.
Many of its buildings date from the 1890s, although frequent fires have taken their toll. In the Gay Nineties,
Jimtown flourished as the supply center for dozens of mines
in the vicinity, and as a stopover on the road to Yosemite.

Over 30 million dollars worth of gold was taken from the
mines around Jamestown, most of it between 1890 and 1916.
During that period, 300 stamps were operating in the
various mills.

Today Jamestown is best known as the home of the
*Sierra Railroad*     Sierra Railroad Company. The Sierra R.R. was incorpor-
*Company*     ated in 1897 by T. S. Bullock, a New York financier,
William Crocker, a San Francisco banker and founder of
the Crocker Bank, and Prince Poniatowski, a European
nobleman. Poniatowski, who was related to the Crockers
by marriage, owned a marble quarry near Columbia. He
stood to gain financially from a rail line running near his
property.

The rails were laid quickly from the main line of the
Central Pacific into the hills. They reached Jimtown in

Oiling the engine.

October 1897. Then there was a brief attempt to run a line to Yosemite, but this was soon abandoned in favor of the Angels Camp Spur, where extensive gold mining operations were crying for more efficient transportation.

The main line ran through Sonora to the Standard Lumber Company's plant at Fassler. This is the same route you may take today.

Not the least of the motives for the construction of the Sierra R.R. was tourism. The Hotel Nevills was a large and luxurious hotel which used to stand next to the train station in Jamestown. It had a roof with up-tilted corners in imitation of the Chinese style. The Nevills served as a rest stop on the way to Yosemite, or to the Calaveras Big Trees, the other tourist attraction of the Golden Hills in the early days.

*Sierra R.R.*

Horse-drawn stage lines operated at the rail heads until 1916, at which time they were replaced by motorized stages; a motorized stage was a cross between a bus and a limousine.

The Sierra R.R. is still the property of the Crocker family. Its glory days have surely passed, but it still does some hauling for the lumber mills and for the Coors distributors. In addition to regular tourist runs, the railway also makes frequent appearances in motion pictures. The line has figured prominently in such films as *High Noon* and *My Little Chickadee*, and television programs like "Petticoat Junction" and "The Wild Wild West."

*Railtown 1897*        Today Railtown 1897 operates a museum and a roundhouse tour in Jamestown. Their rolling stock alone deserve a visit. Recently the regular tourist runs have been expanded to include longer trips with meals or wine tasting.

**Side trip from Jamestown:** The road south leads to one of the major lode mining areas of the Mother Lode system, Quartz Mountain. Here the Heslit-App mine took $6.5 million in gold out of the ground, and other mines pros-

*Quartz*        pered as well. The town of Quartz is on the north side of the hill, while the town of Stent is on the south.

*Stent*        A few traces of the old mining operations remain, although the mines closed over 50 years ago. There are heaps of rocks, called tailings, tunnel openings, and some outbuildings. Stent has a schoolhouse and a graveyard, side by side, a combination repeated too often to be coincidental. Stent was called Poverty Hill during the gold rush because of the poor grade of gold dust that was found there.

*Campo Seco*        Another gold rush town was Campo Seco, which the Americans would have called Dry Diggings. A spur of the Sierra R.R. serves a limestone quarry near here.

**Side trip from Jamestown:** Rawhide Road, on the other side of the highway from Jamestown, offers two interesting walks to the foot of Table Mountain. One leads

*Pulpit Rock*        to Pulpit Rock, a large volcanic formation. The other, slightly more difficult to find, leads to Peppermint Falls. In order to reach the path, drive to the end of Peppermint Falls Road; the path follows the creek to the falls, an easy walk of about a half a mile.

*Peppermint*        Peppermint Falls is hardly spectacular, but it is unusual
*Falls*        because of the odd basalt rocks that compose Table Mountain. At this point, you may want to climb to the top of the mountain, and the climb here is easy enough for a child.

Table Mountain was formed as the result of long-ago volcanic eruptions. It is about 40 miles long and follows the course of an ancient river, called the Proto-Stanislaus by geologists. Its flat top used to be below the summit of surrounding hills, but the hills have eroded over the ages, leaving the harder volcanic formations in the shape of an inverted river valley. Although there is precious little topsoil here, a surprising number of wildflowers bloom here in the spring.

Beyond Peppermint Falls, Rawhide Road continues on into Rawhide Flat, the site of the now nonexistent town of Jefferson and the Rawhide Mine, a large producer during the '90s, worth $6 million to its owners. *Rawhide Flat*

Sonora, called the Queen of the Southern Mines, is the next town along Highway 108. It is the county seat of Tuolumne County. On the right as you enter the town you will see the fairgrounds, where the Mother Lode Round-Up is held in May and the Tuolumne County Fair is held in August. *Sonora*

Across the street from the fairgrounds is the head-quarters of the Stanislaus National Forest. There you can get maps and information about the wildlife and facilities within the forest. *Stanislaus National Forest*

Sonora was a rich goldfield, famous for its large gold nuggets or chispas. Nuggets were sometimes found in the streets long after the gold rush excitement had died down.

Gold was first found here by two brothers of Mexican extraction, Joe and Seamon Cabezut, in 1848. Word spread rapidly in the Mexican community and there were soon many prospectors on the site. Since many of them had come from Sonora, the most northerly of the Mexican provinces, they naturally named their new home after the old one. The Americans called it the Sonoranian Camp.

The Mexicans were soon outnumbered by Americans, and conflicts broke out between the two groups. For awhile they coexisted, but the Mexicans were gradually driven off their claims. A large factor in the accomplishment of this end by the Americans was the passage of the Foreign Miners' Tax of 1851, according to which the foreigners had to pay $20 a month for the privilege of mining American gold. This act caused nearly half the miners to abandon the gold fields. *Foreign Miners' Tax*

Sonora was not unusual in that it housed many saloons, gambling halls, fandango halls and other conveniences designed to part a miner and his gold. It had a bull ring, too. In addition to ordinary Spanish bull fights, a California refinement was the introduction of a grizzly bear to the bull ring. A full-grown grizzly bear is more than a match for any bull, but big bears were hard to find, and many spritely contests were held between smaller bears and larger bulls. Not infrequently the contests were fixed in favor of the bears because of their value, but in general the spectacle must have been an appealing one to the early miners.

When the town became the county seat in 1850, an enterprising delegate to the State Legislature decided that the town should be named after him, so he had the name changed officially to Stewart. The citizenry was so angered at this bit of skullduggery that the name was quickly changed back.

By the end of the Civil War in 1865, Sonora's prosperity was on the wane, but the lumber industry and the road to the Nevada mines kept the town going in hard times.

*Pocket mines*

*Bonanza Mine*

A curious aspect of mining in Tuolumne County was the occurrence of pocket mines. These mines sometimes yielded enormous quantities of gold in a short time. A good example of this was the Bonanza Mine. This mine, located on Piety Hill at the north end of the main street, was supposedly worked out in 1879, but the owners kept it going anyway. One day they struck a pocket of almost pure gold and within 24 hours had shipped $160,000 to the mill.

The arrival of the railroad in 1898 brought renewed prosperity to the town. Its lumber mills were turning out millions of orange crates for the burgeoning California citrus industry. After the First World War, tourists began to discover the foothills, and the local businessmen began to discover the tourists.

Sonora is a bustling community today, but the downtown area retains a surprising number of buildings dating from the gold rush. Even the stores that appear modern are frequently only old stone stores with a coating of stucco and plate glass windows.

*Tuolumne County Historical Museum*

The Old County Jail on Bradford Avenue has been restored and is open to the public as a museum. The Tuolumne County Historical Society is very active. They

Morgan Mansion.

run the museum and have published a number of books on the early history of the county. There is a walking tour available which includes many of the town's picturesque homes. The museum is small and unfortunately inadequate for the size and scope of the collection, of which the gold nuggets and firearms displays are especially worth noting.

The jail itself was built in 1865 as a holding facility for *Jail* minor offenders and those awaiting trial. The Bastille-like structure was used until 1961, which may account for the excellent condition of the building. The front part of the jail was added as a residence for the early sheriffs and their families.

Perhaps the best indicator of the size and importance of a place is its graveyard. The main one in Sonora is large and *Graveyard* filled with impressive monuments. It is at the end of Yaney Street, but it was not the only one. There used to be a Jewish cemetery across the street from the new County Jail. The Masons and the Odd Fellows each had their own cemeteries on Divoll Hill, above Hales and Symons, and the Catholics had a separate graveyard for their faithful. Doubtless the Chinese had their own, where their bodies would rest for awhile before being transported back to China. Even in death, the segregation of races and faiths was rigorous and thorough.

If you walk up Yaney Street from the cemetery, you will pass St. Patrick's Catholic Church, the white church which stands out so prominently when the town is first seen from the west. It was built in 1862.

*County Courthouse*

The main entrance to the County Courthouse is also on Yaney Street. This massive structure was built early in this century to replace a wooden structure on the same site. The main entrance should have faced the main street, but the man who owned the house across the street complained that this would make his street too noisy, so the orientation of the building was altered. The building was constructed to make full use of naturally occurring substances of the county, including the green sandstone in the steps, the grey-grained Columbia marble, and the distinctive yellow bricks. Copper from Copperopolis was used in the main doors and in the clock tower.

*County Recorder's Office*

For those who like old newspapers, the County Recorder's office has a complete collection of all the newspapers from the early days. A beautiful photograph of the Hetch Hetchy Valley prior to 1913 hangs in the Registrar's office.

Continuing on down the same street, you will come to a small park. In this park have been planted several trees native to the Golden Hills. Amateur naturalists can try guessing their names. Our list includes two pines, a cedar, a larch, a fir, and a Big Tree. The Big Tree is now the smallest one, but in 500 years . . .

*Elementary School*

From this park, looking across the town to the other side of the valley, you can see the old Elementary School. It was built in 1902 and resembles the Jefferson mansion at Monticello. Along the main street are many old buildings built of brick and slate to withstand the frequent fires of the nineteenth century. The largest of these is the City Hotel, which has recently been restored to its turn of the century appearance. The original structure of the 1850s was smaller and made of adobe.

*Opera Hall*

Another large building on the main street is the Opera Hall, built in 1886 as a roller skating rink by James Divoll, the owner of the Bonanza Mine. Presently it is occupied by a garage, but soon it will become vacant again and it faces an uncertain future.

At the north end of the main street are the Odd Fellows

Hall, the Yosemite House, and the Red Church, St. James
Episcopal Church, built in 1859. Across the street from the
Red Church is the town's most spectacular Victorian Gin-
gerbread, built in the 1890s by the town's wealthiest
businessman, S. S. Bradford, whose mills turned out the
doors and windows of many of California's finest old
homes.

*The Red Church*

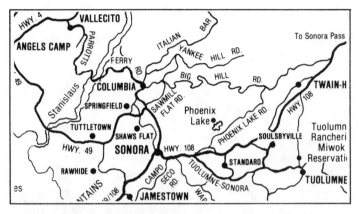

**Side trip from Sonora:** On the way out of town via
Highway 49 to the north, you will come to an intersection.
To the right is Columbia Way, to the left is the road to
Shaws Flat, while the highway straight ahead is the fastest
way to Columbia.

*Columbia*

Columbia Way used to be the main road to Columbia.
The route runs past the residence of J. B. Curtin, who ran
for Governor against Hiram Johnson in 1908. The stream is
Woods Creek. This road was reportedly lined with miner's
cabins all the way to Columbia. Perhaps $50 million worth
of placer gold was taken out of this creek, surely one of the
wealthiest streams anywhere.

Shaws Flat Road leads past the high school. The playing
field was once a farm called Holden's Gardens, where fruit
and vegetables were grown for the miners. Holden was a
Texas gunfighter who had to protect his property from the
miners with his guns. He eventually lost the battle, and a
gold nugget weighing 28 pounds was dug up there.

Highway 49 leads to Columbia, the Gem of the Southern
Mines. Take the turn at Parrotts Ferry Road, and the
growing concentration of fast food stands and antique

stores will tell you when you are nearing the town. The large boulders along the road are the result of hydraulic mining. This was possibly the richest gold rush town, with a production of between 90 and 150 million dollars worth of gold.

At their peak, the gold fields around Columbia were being worked by 15,000 miners. In 1854, it was the second largest city in the state, and had lost out to Sacramento in the vote for the state capital by only two votes in the legislature. It had four banks and 143 Faro banks. The built-up portion of the main street was about twice as long as it is

Cabin near Squabbletown.

now; the northern portion was destroyed by the fire of 1857 and never rebuilt.

During the gold rush, Columbia was the largest town in the area, but it had a number of satellite towns which today are true ghost towns—that is, they have only a name on the map or a couple of old ruins to show where they once stood. For the record, they were Gold Springs, Italian Bar, Yankee Hill, Martinez, Sawmill Flat, Squabbletown, Union Hill, and Springfield.

After the initial rush was over, Columbia kept going with lode mines in the area. There are dozens of small mines nearby, including the Gold Bug, which is visited by an organized tour. The water companies, with their massive water projects, permitted the extensive use of hy-

Replica of a miner's cabin at Columbia.

draulic mining techniques, which in turn were responsible for lowering the ground around Columbia at least ten feet, and in many places leaving deep pits and exposed boulders.

The buildings of Columbia were left to the elements for fifty years after the last mines closed. Many were undermined by miners digging under their foundations. The bricks of others were carried away for barbecues and retaining walls. By the time the town was made into an historic park in 1945, most of the structures lay in ruins. Two of the best-preserved buildings, judging from early photographs, are the Wells Fargo Building at one end of the main street and the St. Charles Saloon at the other.

*Wells Fargo Building*

*St. Charles Saloon*

In 1945, Columbia finally became the state capital, for one day, at the occasion of the dedication of the park. The chief speaker at the ceremony was Governor Earl Warren.

Today many of the buildings of the old gold rush town have been reconstructed. The points of interest include the Fallon House theater, which has been restored to provide a stage for the University of the Pacific's summer theatrical productions. Since space is very limited, reservations are a must. Old-time melodramas, at the other end of the street

*Fallon House theater*

in the Fandango Hall, are performed regularly during the summertime and no reservations are needed there.

*Columbia Gazette building*

The Columbia Gazette building houses a museum of newspaper memorabilia in its basement. The Wells Fargo building has many of its original furnishings, including a scale said to have weighed $50 million worth of gold dust. The D. O. Mills Building next door was one of the first branches of what later came to be called the Bank of California.

The Columbia museum is not large, but it doesn't have to be; the whole town is a museum, filled with priceless and irreplaceable objects. In the forefront of these must be counted the antique fire engines. Every year at the end of May the town holds a firemen's muster to display these old machines in action. The event brings out other machines from throughout the state.

*City Hotel*

The City Hotel has been restored and now houses a fully-equipped bar and a French restaurant, as well as a few hotel rooms. The miner's cabin at the end of the main street speaks volumes about the life in the mining camps, even for the most prosperous miners.

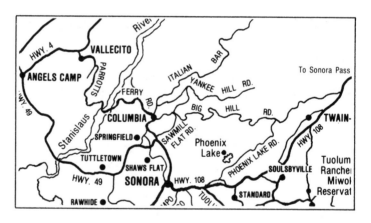

*Gold Springs*

*Vallecito*

**Side trip from Columbia:** Parrotts Ferry Road leads past Gold Springs, a modern development of luxury homes, down into the Stanislaus River Canyon. The views are excellent, including the ones of the old marble quarries. Under construction at the river is a new bridge which will make the trip to Vallecito shorter and more enjoyable.

**Side trip from Columbia:** Italian Bar Road leads into the rugged back country of Stanislaus National Forest, suitable for exploration by off-the-road vehicles.

*Stanislaus National Forest*

**Side trip from Columbia:** Yankee Hill Road leads past a campground, a small winery and the site of Yankee Hill, an old mining camp. From Yankee Hill, a loop may be made by taking Sawmill Flat Road to the right. Along this road is Columbia College, a two-year college in the State College system. Here there are a number of things to see, including a Miwok roundhouse near the entrance to the parking lot; a nature walk through an area that was extensively mined with hydraulic hoses; San Diego Reservoir, where water from the Stanislaus River is stored for use in Columbia; and a library well-stocked with books on the history of the Golden Hills.

*Columbia College*

Sawmill Flat Road also passes Martinez, where Joaquin Murrieta was supposed to have worked for Dona Martinez in a Mexican gambling casino. The sawmill for which the flat was named has long since vanished.

*Martinez*

## Highway 49 — Shaws Flat, Springfield, and Tuttletown

Not far beyond the turn-off for Columbia, the Shaws Flat-Springfield Road crosses Highway 49. At the intersection is the huge quarry where aggregates are mined. Aggregates are minerals which are not bound together in ores and which may be refined by crushing. Some idea of the noise caused by a gold mill may be realized on a day when the aggregates mill is running.

Shaws Flat is a small town about a mile south of the highway. It has a fascinating history, but a humble appearance. The oldest building, the Mississippi House, dates from the early days of the gold rush. James Fair, who later built the Fairmont Hotel in San Francisco, mined in this camp as a young man. The town thrived during the Table Mountain excitement of 1857. There was a lot of surface gold, too, but the water level was too high to make deep drifts feasible.

*Shaws Flat*

*Mississippi House*

Another interesting spot is the graveyard, and across from it, the old schoolhouse. The school bell is mounted in front of the new school building. This was the miner's alarm bell and the volunteer fire department's bell.

*Springfield*

About a mile north of the highway is the small town of Springfield. The town was prosperous by virtue of its natural springs. Columbia was a dry diggings, and the ore had to be brought to Springfield to be washed. A marker is in the middle of the town square, which used to lined with shops and houses in the Spanish style. We know this because the town was one of the few that was incorporated during the gold rush, and maps were made of the lots. About 4,000 people lived here, and it was a law-abiding town. The first building was reputedly a church.

One of the famous residents of the town was Dona Josefa Balmesada, a Mexican National who had aided the American cause during the Mexican-American War. After the war she had to flee her homeland. She eventually settled here and set up a mining company with other Mexicans.

The single stone building in the town has had many uses over the years. It originally housed the Methodist Church.

The springs may be seen at the north end of the square, underneath the bridge. The fresh water is used by a trout farm.

The land between Springfield and Columbia was so rocky that for a long time nothing could be done with it. During the 1930s an airport was built here which is operating today. Yosemite Airlines has scheduled flights to Oakland and a fly-over of Yosemite—a truly unique and spectacular way to see the wonders of the Golden Hills.

*Tuttletown*

Highway 49 continues on to Tuttletown, at the foot of Jackass Hill. It was an early settlement, perhaps identical with the oft-mentioned Jackass Gulch which was one of the earliest mining camps in this part of the Mother Lode. Its modern name is that of an early judge.

Sad to say, the Schwerer store, the last remnant of the gold rush town, is crumbling into ruin and will soon have disappeared altogether. Neither Mark Twain nor Bret Harte ever clerked there, but its loss is regrettable nevertheless.

The other place where Mark Twain never stayed was the

Mark Twain Cabin. This replica of the original cabin belonging to the Gillis brothers was built in 1926, 16 years after the famous humorist's death. Its godfather was W. J. Loring, who made a fortune by opening up the Plymouth mine in Amador County and the Carson Hill mine across the river from the cabin.

*Mark Twain Cabin*

Tuttletown was remarkable for the talent that did live there, as well as the writers who were just passing through. Among the latter we must count Mark Twain and Bret Harte. Another transient was John Rollin Ridge, who wrote the story of Joaquin Murrieta under the name Yellow Bird. He was a full-blooded Cherokee whose abilities were fully suited to the task of memorializing the Robin Hood of El Dorado, Joaquin.

*Mark Twain Bret Harte*

Among the residents was Prentice Mulford, a journalist who was well-known by the pseudonym of Dogberry. The frontier journalists had no literary illusions when they adopted pen names; they were merely protecting their own hides. Every editor kept a six-gun in his desk to protect himself against the irate public. When Mark Twain took his pseudonym, the Civil War was raging in the East and causing much turmoil in the West.

One of Tuttletown's contributions to the county was the first lending library. It was a private affair, but some of its books are still being used in the Tuolumne Public Library.

Beyond Tuttletown lies Archie Stevenot Bridge with its splendid view of the Stanislaus River Canyon, and Calaveras County to the north.

*Archie Stevenot Bridge*

## Highway 108—Sonora to Sonora Pass

The highway between Jamestown and Soulsbyville is one of the least attractive roads in the Golden Hills, which is a shame because the countryside here is so often strikingly beautiful. Not only have buildings been built which obstruct the view, but cars entering and leaving the highway pose a traffic hazard for the unwary. However, efforts are being made to alleviate both problems.

The areas to the north and south of this road are quite attractive and may be explored without much difficulty. The first turn-off, to the right, is at Tuolumne Road, just

after the road crosses Sullivan's Creek. The other, a half
mile past Tuolumne Road, is at Phoenix Lake Road on the
left.

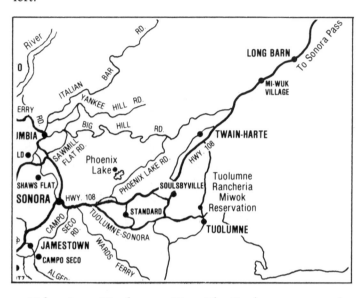

**Side trip to Tuolumne City:** The Tuolumne crosses the
track of the Sierra Railroad before heading up the hill to
*Fassler*   Fassler, the location of the Pickering Lumber Mill, which is
the largest single industry in the county.

You can get a pretty good idea of the operation from the
road. There are stacks of logs lying ready for milling. In the
old days these logs would be floating in a mill pond to keep
them from cracking in the sun, but today they are sprayed
with water instead. This plant has a capacity of 40,000
board feet of lumber daily. Operating around the clock
(except Sundays), the plant turns out 120 million board feet
every year. On Sunday you can see the rigs parked in long
rows near the entrance gate. The rest of the week they are
out on the road, shuttling back and forth between the
logging sites and the mill.

*Standard*   The ghost town of Standard is about a mile north on the
Standard Road. It is an example of the maxim that the
more things change, the more they remain the same, for the
town was only recently abandoned but its destruction
followed a pattern that has been going on in the Golden
Hills for over a century.

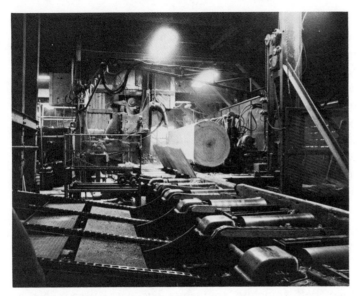

Sugar Pine being milled at Fassler.

Typical of the early stories is that of the town of Curtis Creek, which was not far from Standard, although precisely where it lay is anybody's guess. When the Curtis Creek ditch was completed, bringing water to the previously dry diggings at Algerine, the entire town was dismantled and taken to the new site. Algerine in its turn was abandoned by the miners when its deposits ran out.

*Curtis Creek*

*Algerine*

Standard was a bustling company town in the early decades of this century, the kind of place where all the inhabitants worked for the same boss. There was no real need for money, since all supplies could be purchased at the company store, nor was there any problem of youth unemployment, since the youngsters all went to work for the company as soon as they were old enough. The old company towns like Standard offered a kind of security which is hard to find in today's society.

Time finally caught up with the town in the early 1970s when Pickering Corporation was acquired by the conglomerate Fibreboard, Inc. The new owners decided the town was unprofitable and proceeded to sell it. The last house was moved out in 1976. Now Standard has a school, a post office, a church, and several company office buildings—but no houses and no people.

The town also has a little-used spur of the Sierra Railroad. This situation makes Standard perfect for use in motion pictures and television productions, and it is seen frequently, though generally with some other name. Recently the town was used in a sequence for a television program about runaway slaves in the South.

Continuing along Tuolumne Road, you will pass over the shoulder of Buckhorn Mountain and down into the pleasant town of Tuolumne. As you approach the town you will see the West Side and Cherry Valley Railway, an amusement park which seeks to revive the era before World War I, when the mines were in operation, the trains were running, and a new invention called the automobile was making a lot of noise.

*West Side and Cherry Valley Railroad*

This theme park is the brainchild of Glen Bell, who is building it with the proceeds he earned from the sale of his Taco Bell franchise company. The park already has a narrow gauge steam engine in operation, and they have reconstructed the old roundhouse and the mill pond. Plans for the future entail construction of five theme villages: a Chinese town, a Mexican town, a logging town, a mining town, and an Indian camp, each with its own shops and restaurants. Connecting these five villages will be the various forms of transport used during the period: a steam-driven train, antique cars and buses, horse-drawn vehicles, and others. The center of attraction will be the restored West Side Mill.

*Tuolumne*

The little town of Tuolumne is surrounded by tree-covered mountains. Its salutary atmosphere once made it the location of a sanitorium. The air is cool and crisp, scented with pine and cooled by the 2,600-foot elevation. The first residents on the site were Franklin and Elizabeth Summers, who set up residence here during the east belt gold rush of 1857.

The "east belt" was a gold bearing quartz vein system similar to the Mother Lode system ten miles west. Productive mines of the east belt were located at Cherokee, Confidence, Soulsbyville (with both the Soulsby and Draper mines), Arrastraville and Summersville—for so the town was called at first, by the sometime-custom in the goldfields of naming the towns after a female resident. The mine here was called the Eureka.

Mining was a boom or bust industry, and the town of Summersville had its ups and downs. In the 1890s an attempt was made to capitalize on the town's natural beauty and its proximity to Yosemite National Park. A large resort hotel, called the Turnback Inn, was built on Turnback Creek, and the arrival of the railroad was eagerly awaited. The Hetch Hetchy and Yosemite Valley Railroad was incorporated and the town prepared for a boom. But by the time the Sierra Railroad reached Turnback Creek in 1901, logging interests had gained control of the line, and a mill town, called Carter's, was established. In 1903, the same year the Turnback Inn was destroyed by fire, there were 1,800 workers employed by the mill, and the West Side and Cherry Valley was a logging line.

*Summersville*

*Carter's*

It was a narrow-gauge line, and one of the crookedest anywhere. Along one 19-mile stretch there was not a single spot where a seven-car train was entirely straight, and several where it formed an S-curve. Before the line was stopped in 1949, it stretched 72 miles (not counting the numerous spurs) and reached within a mile and a half of the Yosemite Park boundary.

In the early 1960s, the West Side mill operations were shut down—the logging industry was switching from railroad to trucking—and the employees of the Pickering Corporation, which at that time owned both the West Side mill and the one at Fassler, went on strike to protect the closing and loss of jobs. The strike was a violent one. It ended in 1962 with the burning of the West Side mill, after which there was nothing left to strike about.

There was also not much left to employ the residents of Tuolumne City, which went into a rapid decline. It is hoped that the West Side and Cherry Valley Railway will provide the town with needed economic input.

*Tuolumne City*

Besides the park, Tuolumne has a few charming homes, a municipal swimming pool and playground. It is a good place to escape the summer's heat. Because of its location next to the National Forest, Tuolumne is a good jumping off point for side trips. One road leads north toward

*Twain-Harte*     Twain-Harte; a second leads east toward Cherry Lake and Hetch Hetchy; a third will take you south to Wards Ferry and Groveland.

**Side trip from Tuolumne:** The Confidence Road leads
*Tuolumne*     past the Tuolumne Rancheria, one of the few Miwok
*Rancheria*     reservations left. The entire population of the Sierra Miwok tribe is now only 150. What it may once have been is hard to guess, but it is estimated that the population of the Indian tribes in 1900 was only one-tenth of what it was in 1800. The decrease was due to disease, absorption into the white population, and wholesale murder. There is a roundhouse on this reservation.

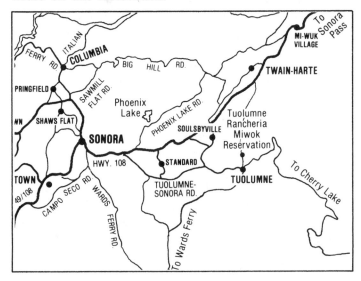

Shortly past the Rancheria is the Cherokee Road. On this
*Sonka's*     road is Sonka's Apple Ranch, 40 acres of apples, pears and
*Apple Ranch*     other trees. The section of the Golden Hills between three and four thousand feet above sea level was once known as the apple belt. There is no doubt, on the evidence presented by the few ranches remaining in this region, that the apples grown here are far better tasting than their flatland counterparts. The apple harvest begins about midsummer, and apples are available at the ranch until well into autumn. The freshly pressed cider is especially delicious.

The Confidence road leads back to Highway 108 near Twain-Harte.

Thirteen-mile Creek.

**Side trip from Tuolumne:** The narrow-gauge railway no longer runs between Tuolumne and Cherry Valley, but some idea of the trip may be experienced by driving along the winding, well-paved road which follows approximately the same route as the old railway. The road is slow going, but there are numerous side roads for the adventurous, as well as picnic and hiking spots. The road continues all the way to Hetch Hetchy past some truly magnificent and isolated countryside.

**Side trip from Tuolumne:** The road to the south begins by passing through pleasant, tree-shaded country lands. These are followed by rolling, oak-studded hillsides. In the spring, this is an excellent wildflower route, while in the summer it will lead you down to the Tuolumne River at Wards Ferry, where boats can be launched.

Phoenix Lake Road leads through countryside quite different from that around Tuolumne Road. Here the elevation rises more rapidly, and the road is lined with large suburban homes. Several suburban developments co-exist here with some large oak trees and old farm houses.

The roads can get a little difficult to follow at times, so a map is imperative. Among the things you might want to see are Crystal Falls with its subdivision; Phoenix Lake with its golf course and country club; and Kuen Mill Road with its old stone farmhouse. Big Hill Road leads past the Sierra Glen Apple Ranch on its way over the hills to Columbia. It is possible to reach Twain-Harte by the back roads without too much difficulty, and this might be the better route for those who can spare the time.

*Crystal Falls*

*Phoenix Lake*

After the Phoenix Lake turn-off, Highway 108 has fewer and fewer shops. It passes near but not through the old towns of Standard and Mono Vista. Soulsbyville was a mining town famous for its tranquility. All the miners there came from Cornwall in England. They were family men who were not inclined to indulge themselves, as the less settled placer miners did, in gambling and carousing.

*Soulsbyville*

The growing resort of Twain-Harte is located on the site of an old Miwok encampment. When a white settler wanted to farm their land, all he had to do was tell them to go and they left. So much for the savagery of the California Indians.

*Twain-Harte*

In 1862 the Williams Ranch became the site of the lower toll gate on the Sonora-Mono wagon road, built to carry supplies across the Sierra to the new silver and gold mining districts in Nevada. The road followed approximately the same course as the present highway.

*Williams Ranch*

In the beginning the main transport along the road was by oxcart. Since oxen could travel only three miles a day, their use required relay stations to be set up at frequent intervals along the road.

In 1926 the Williams Ranch was subdivided into parcels for vacation cabins. At the time there was an effort to popularize the Mother Lode on the basis of its literary legacy—just as the authors themselves had built their careers on the legends of the gold rush. So, while they were looking for a name for the new town, they hit upon the idea of naming it after not one but two famous authors, Mark Twain and Bret Harte.

The main street takes its name from yet another literary figure, Joaquin Miller, the poet of the Sierra.

*Joaquin Miller*

The town is quite ordinary, despite such impressive

pretensions. It has a beautiful location under the pines at a 3,600-foot elevation. Like many other modern subdivisions, it is equipped with all sorts of recreational conveniences, including two golf courses and a small lake. It has easy access to the National Forest for off-the-road vehicles and hikers.

Highway 108 climbs rapidly above Twain-Harte, passing by a number of towns which have long histories and whose recent development has been rapid. Mi-Wuk Village subdivision was started by Harry Hoffer, the candy manufacturer, but no Indians reside there currently. Long Barn's long barn was used by the ox drivers on their way to Nevada, but it burned down long ago.

*Mi-Wuk Village*

There is a Forest Headquarters at Pinecrest, which is an extremely popular resort. During the summer Pinecrest campground is the only one in the Stanislaus National Forest where reservations are required. It has a large alpine lake and is located in the midst of wilderness.

In the winter alpine skiers crowd Dodge Ridge. Others, not so adventurous, come merely to watch, or else to take

*Dodge Ridge*

advantage of the closest snow to the Bay Area to try out their toboggans and build snowmen.

In the winter the highway is closed not far beyond Pinecrest, but in the summer the whole recreational area is open for use. For those who are only driving, there are spectacular vistas, a forest of dwarf trees, and the columns of the giants—huge rock formations of volcanic origin.

Sonora Pass is 9,628 feet above sea level. On the other side lie Nevada, Bridgeport, and the fascinating ghost town of Bodie.

# Part Four:

# Highway 26/Highway 4—Calaveras County

Calaveras County was one of the original 27 counties established by the state legislature in 1850. In 1806 the area had been visited by the Moraga expedition, who discovered a large number of unburied bodies near the Calaveras River. In Spanish the name means "skulls."

*Calaveras River*

Just what those skulls were doing there has been a subject for dispute ever since. The Spaniards believed they were seeing the result of a large battle, possibly between the hill tribes and the valley tribes over the right to fish for salmon in the river. However, contemporary accounts place the number of bodies at as high as 3,000, and such a large battle seems unlikely.

At that time, just 30 years after the Spaniards had begun to civilize the Indians in the northern part of the state, natives were dying more as a result of epidemics than from any other cause. It is likely that the 3,000 people lying unburied there had been wiped out by disease. This would explain why they were not buried.

Highway 26 follows one of the early routes into the county from Stockton. Charles Weber, the founder of Stockton, first discovered gold in this region, along the banks of the Mokelumne River in 1848. Many of the first settlers in the region were military men, members of Colonel Stevenson's California brigade. After fighting in the Mexican-American War, these men were mustered out

*Charles Weber*

in Alta California (Upper California) so that they might provide the nucleus for American settlement of the region.

Since many of the other settlers in the region were Mexicans who had fought on the Mexican side during the recent conflict, it is not surprising that racial conflict was particularly intense here.

*Miwoks*

Captain Weber was unusual among the American settlers in that he enjoyed good relations with the Miwoks. Hayakumnes, known to the Spanish as Jose Jesus, the head chief of the Miwoks north of the Tuolumne River, went into partnership with Weber to ensure the safety of mining operations from Indian attack.

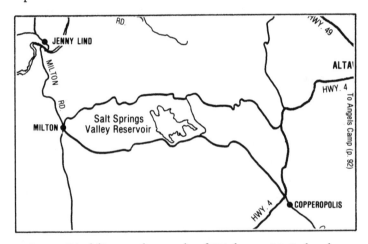

*Jenny Lind*

Jenny Lind lies to the south of Highway 26. It has been bypassed by the highway and by progress, though it once lay along the main road to San Andreas and Mokelumne Hill. Gold was discovered there in 1849. As there was no convenient source of water, Jenny Lind was a "dry diggin's" before it got its permanent name.

Jenny Lind, the Swedish Nightingale, was neither the best soprano of her day nor the most widely traveled, but she was the best known. She owed her popularity to the genius of P. T. Barnum, who could promote a class act as easily as a big elephant or a little man named Tom Thumb.

Ms. Lind made two concert tours in the U.S. during the 1850s, but she never consented to tour the American West, for the simple reason that it was completely uncivilized. But her fame must have reached the miners here. Perhaps, as they had no female residents to honor in the naming of their town, they decided to name it after one who lived far away, whom one or more of them may have seen perform.

Although Ms. Lind never came to the gold fields, many other actors and actresses did. Edwin Booth (the brother of the assassin) got his start here; he claimed that if he ever missed a line in his recitations of Shakespeare, someone in his audience was sure to correct him.

Many other musicians and actors visited the Golden Hills to entertain the miners, who were both wealthy and starved for entertainment. Many popular songs of the era were written for this audience of rough pioneers, among them "Sweet Betsy from Pike" and "Clementine."   *Entertainment*

One of the most popular songs was sung to the tune of Auld Lang Syne. Written by Samuel C. Upham, it was called "Days of Forty-nine":
> "Oh my heart is filled
> With the days of yore
> And oft I do repine
> For the days of old
> And the days of gold
> And the days of forty-nine."

This poem typifies not only the feelings of many '49ers afterwards, but also the spirit of the time while it was going on. It is reported that in the first year of the gold rush there was no crime, no strife, and no violence. Good feelings were everywhere, because any man with a shovel could make a living with a minimum of effort.

**Side trip from Jenny Lind: Milton and Copperpolis via Milton Road (J14):** If these side trips had names, this one would have to be the bad man special. Milton, now a ranching community, was the end of the railroad in 1871. The stagecoach that brought gold shipments to the railroad from Sonora and Columbia had the unwanted distinction of having suffered the most hold-ups of any line in California.   *Milton*

Whether the road between Milton and Copperopolis presently follows the old stage route very closely is hard to determine. It is rather narrow, and there are some places so removed from signs of modern civilization that you almost expect to see a stagecoach around the next turn.

The land around Milton once produced excellent wheat crops, but its productivity was destroyed in only a few years by poor farming methods. Now this land is almost barren, supporting only a sparse crop of hay.

*Salt Springs Reservoir*

The Salt Springs Reservoir lies between Milton and Copperopolis. It is a small lake, but it has a picnic area and a boat ramp. The shallow waters are treacherous in a high wind.

Smelter ruins at Copperopolis.

*Copperopolis*

*Hiram Hughes*

The sleepy town of Copperopolis, called Copper for convenience, is unusual as a mining town because gold was never important here. Copper was king. The founder of the town was Hiram Hughes, a hard-luck prospector who had been prospecting in the Golden Hills, in Virginia City and in the Washoe Mountains of Nevada for years without much success. Hughes came back to the area around Copper because he had noted similarities between the mountains here and the Washoes.

*Quail Hill Mine*

In 1860 Hughes sent some ore samples to be assayed for their silver content. They contained copper worth 120 dollars a ton. The first mine was the Quail Hill mine, and the timing of the discovery was fortuitous. The Civil War in the East created a large demand for copper, which is a component of brass used in shell casings and armaments. Copperopolis was strongly pro-Union during the war, and Union soldiers were garrisoned here to protect the mines.

After the Civil War was over, the bottom fell out of the copper market, all the mines closed, and Copperopolis was practically a ghost town. But by 1902, the demand had risen again and the mines were reopened. The period of prosperity lasted until the early '50s, when the mines closed down again. This time another substance was found nearby, asbestos, and the town has not been abandoned altogether.

There were once 10,000 people living here, but only a handful make it their home today. Due to the recent date of the shut-down of the mines (in comparison with other places which closed down in 1916), some of the mill buildings may be seen in the town, although these are disappearing as well.

Most of the copper mines were in the mountains to the west of the town, along Highway 4 in the vicinity of Telegraph City. The city was a mining town that got its name from the telegraph wires which ran through it between Stockton and Sonora. Highway 4 is a slow route back to Stockton and the Central Valley.

*Telegraph City*

Also in the vicinity of Copperopolis is Lake Tulloch, on the O'Byrnes Ferry Road. Tulloch is a recreational reservoir where there are a number of small subdivisions.

*Lake Tulloch*

In order to get to the site of most of the stage hold-ups on the Sonora-Milton line, you have to take a detour through the Bar XX subdivision. The old route ran along the Reynolds, or Lavilla Ferry Road, which only exists in spots. In Bar XX, there is a lookout from Fowler Peak from which the Melones Reservoir may be seen. The Peak is 2,900 feet high and located at the end of Stallion Way.

*Fowler Peak*

But the place where the highwaymen called out, "Stand and deliver!" was Funk Hill, not far from the end of Filly Lane (off Appaloosa Road). Here the old road climbed over a ridge and the horses slowed to a walk. This was the spot where Black Bart robbed his second gold shipment in 1877, and his last in 1884.

*Funk Hill*

Black Bart led a double, or even a triple life. In San Francisco he was a respectable citizen, Charles Bolton, who apparently had independent means. When he went on voyages he used the name Bowles. He was not much of a horseman, for he always used the stagecoach on his business trips.

*Black Bart*

His business was stopping coaches and demanding a toll for their continued safe passage. His name for business purposes was taken from a note left at the scene of one of his early crimes, which read,

"I've labored long and hard for bread,
For honor and for riches,
But on my toes too long you've tread,
You fine-haired sons of bitches.
[signed] Black Bart, the Po-8 [poet]"

Bart's literary career was brief, but his other business activities lasted seven years, during which he committed 26 or more robberies. During his last robbery, at Funk Hill, he was surprised in the act of jimmying the strong box by a hunter who was coming to meet the stage at that point. Bart escaped, but a laundry mark on a handkerchief he dropped at the scene led to his eventual apprehension.

Black Bart stood trial in San Andreas. During his trial it was brought out in his defense that the shotgun with which he committed his crimes was never loaded, and that he had never fired a shot nor injured a soul during his career. In view of these mitigating circumstances, he was given a light sentence, six years at San Quentin. After his release Bart left California and vanished.

Perhaps the development of the New Melones Reservoir will make Funk Hill accessible to the public and renovate the Reynolds Ferry Road. At least the hill will remain above water when the lake is filled.

*New Melones Reservoir*

The New Melones Reservoir has been completed, but it will be several years before the developments along its shoreline are undertaken. Only then will it be known whether the proponents of the dam were correct in their assessment of the recreational and agricultural needs of this part of the state.

The New Melones Project caused one of the fiercest battles between conservationists and developers since the Hetch Hetchy Project in 1913. During the intense media campaign that accompanied the initiative referendum, the opponents of the dam were characterized by the proponents as a groups of river rafting companies who selfishly desired to keep the river for themselves. However, this could not have been the case, since the rafting companies are all extremely small businesses which could not possibly have raised the money necessary for opposition to the project.

The project has a great deal to offer in its behalf. It will provide 285,000 acre-feet of water annually for irrigation purposes. The water released will generate a large supply of clean hydro-electric energy. Up to 3,000 acres of park land will be developed, not only around the lake itself, but also down river, where the unique riparian forest will be preserved, an area which provides nesting and foraging habitat for dozens of different species of birds and mammals.

Although several miles of white-water rapids will be eliminated by the dam, a short all-year kayaking course will be established near Knights Ferry—it may even help to improve America's miserable Olympic record in this exciting sport. An estimated three million visitors will eventually use the combined recreational facilities of the lake each year.

*Knights Ferry*

In addition, work will be done along the river below the dam to restore gravel beds which salmon formerly used for spawning. That, together with the added purity and lower temperature of water from the reservoir, should restore the salmon run in the Stanislaus within a few years.

In the interest of preserving rare and endangered species, no matter how insignificant they may at first appear, the dam builders have removed a colony of harvestmen (daddy long-legs) from a cave which will be flooded by the dam to an abandoned mine tunnel within the boundaries of the National Forest. These strange creatures look like white spiders and are nearly blind due to their habitat in the dark recesses of caves. Incidentally, the new Melones Recreation area will include about 60 known limestone caves. This is the largest karst (cave region) west of the Continental Divide.

*Limestone caves*

On the debit side of the ledger, the new lake will inundate the site of Melones and other early mining camps at the bottom of the Stanislaus canyon. However, these sites were neither extensive nor unique, and it is possible that the preparations for the dam will reveal more artifacts than it will cover up.

The New Melones Project seems to be beneficial rather than detrimental to the environment, although the future will tell us more about that. But without the strident activity of environmentalists and the concern of the people of California, the new lake would most assuredly have been an ecological disaster.

Past Bar XX, Highway 4 leads to Angels Camp, to which we will turn our attention later.

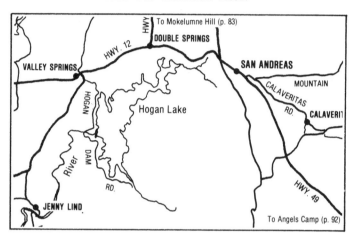

*New Hogan Dam*

Highway 26 north of Jenny Lind has seen a great deal of new development since the completion of the New Hogan Dam in 1964. The observation point near the dam may be reached by taking the Silver Rapids Road to the right about three miles north of the Milton turn-off. The Fiddleneck day-use area and Acorn Campground are reached by the Hogan Dam Road in Valley Springs.

*Acorn Campground*

The names of these campsites are good ones. The oak is the most characteristic tree of the lower foothills. Its spreading limbs provide welcome shade on those summer days when the mercury in the thermometer rises rapidly to 100° and then gets lost. The fiddleneck is a common yellow wildflower with a distinctive shape: the top of the stem, covered with tiny flowers, curls over like the scroll-work on a fiddle.

*Hogan Lake*

Hogan Lake provides a setting in the rolling foothills for every conceivable outdoor and aquatic activity. La Contenta Country Club along Highway 26 adds a golf course to the list of possible pastimes.

Just a short drive along the highway to the east of Valley Springs will bring you to Double Springs. Once the county seat of Calaveras County, the old town vanished with its placer gold. The county records were moved to Jackson in 1850.

*Double Springs*

The town that took the county seat away from Jackson was Mokelumne Hill, which lies northeast of Double Springs along Highway 26. For awhile, Mok Hill was the

*Mokelumne Hill*

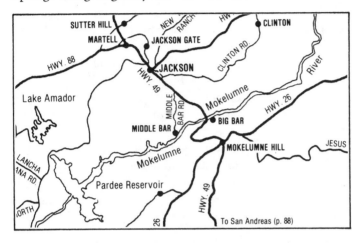

most prosperous (and most riotous) town in the county. Gold was discovered at Big Bar on the Mokelumne River in 1848 by members of the Stevenson Regiment.

*Big Bar*

The area was first inhabited by a tribe of Miwoks who were called the Mokelumne (pronounced Muh-col'-ummy), which means people of Mokel in the native dialect. In his treatise on the California Indians, Kroeber states that Mokel was an Indian village near Lockeford.

Because of Chief Hayakumnes' friendship with Charles Weber, the tribal organization of this area is better known than in other sections of the Golden Hills. The chief of the Mokelumnes was named Polo, while he and the other local chiefs were under the jurisdiction of Hayakumnes.

Mok Hill began to grow as a town shortly after gold was discovered on Stockton Hill in 1848. All the hills surrounding the town were found to have large subterranean deposits which could be exploited by means of drifts or tunnels. This was still placer gold, however, and did not necessitate the construction of mills or arrastras.

The town grew rapidly. Law and order were quickly shattered by the influx of miners from every race and dozens of nations. The French trappers had had an outpost in Happy Valley before gold was discovered so it was only natural that they should come here in large numbers. The revolution of 1848 in France made it convenient for the French government to send soldiers to the gold fields. These were irregular troops who had been responsible for the bloody quelling of the Parisians, so their presence was a definite embarrassment to the government when the war ended.

*French Hill*

The French discovered gold at French Hill in 1851. The discovery precipitated a mob action by the Americans, who tried to seize the French claims. They were incensed when the Frenchmen raised the Tricolor on the hill above their claims.

Another element in the population was the blacks. Some of them were former slaves freed by their masters when California became a state. Some were runaways, while others had promised to send the price of their freedom to their masters in the south out of their earnings in the gold fields.

In 1851, according to the story, a black man walked into Mok Hill and asked some miners where he could prospect for gold. They thought it was a good joke to direct him toward a hill where gold had not been found, for which he thanked them and left. After a few days the fellow returned, laden with gold nuggets. His reappearance caused a shock among the miners, who had been laughing about the joke they played on him. In a few minutes, the whole town was in turmoil. Men were milling around, getting together their gear, bargaining for fast horses, closing down their shops. In another few minutes, the town was deserted except for the man who had caused the commotion, who didn't understand what all the excitement was about.

The men all rushed for the hill to make their claims and start digging. One eyewitness said the hill looked like ants were swarming over it. Naturally, they named it Nigger Hill.

*Chilenos*

The Chileños also worked in this area. Like the other minorities, the French and the Mexicans, the Chileños had their own bars, their own hotels, their own protective associations and their own hospitals. They also brought their own social system, with its two classes of masters and peons. Before long, the Americans in the town thought this was too much like slavery for their liking. It was not that they opposed the holding of human chattels; far from it. It was only that there was a law against slaves holding claims: the master could have his claim worked by slave labor, if he liked, but he could have only one claim.

This law was one of those instituted by Colonel Stevenson himself, who was the town's first alcalde and also wrote the first mining laws in the state.

The Americans tried to force the Chileños off their claims in 1849, but the Chileños were organized and well able to defend themselves. Armed with court orders from a judge sympathetic to their side (he was a Southerner and pro-slavery), the Chileños repelled the Americans and took two of them hostage. This only made the Americans angry, so they got their own court order (from a Northerner) and tried to enforce it in a body.

The Americans captured a group of Chileños, hanged three of them from the nearest tree and had the others flogged. That ended the Chile War, but bad feelings per-   *Chile War*
sisted for years, with fist fights, free-for-alls, and murders.

There was a period of 17 weeks when at least one man was killed every Saturday night as a result of violence. This earned Mokelumne Hill its reputation as the roughest town in the Golden Hills and probably contributed to its decline. In 1852, in a disputed election, Mok Hill succeeded Jackson as the county seat. The feud between the populations north and south of the Mokelumne River had many similarities to the dissension between the Northern and the Southern states which would soon erupt into the Civil War. Not long after Mok Hill became the county seat, Calaveras County lost the territory north of the river and Amador County was formed.

It was about this time that Joaquin Murrieta became a   *Joaquin Murrieta*
folk hero to the Mexican population in the Golden Hills. The Mexican peasants were the most despised element in the population, with the possible exception of the Miwoks. Not only did the Mexican peasantry have to endure their

mistreatment at the hands of the Americans, they also had to submit to insults and injustices from the upper class Mexicans, the sons of the landed aristocracy.

Joaquin Murrieta was the avenger of wrongs done to all Mexicans, not only to himself. Naturally, he hung out at Mok Hill, where criminals were commonplace and violence was the norm. It is said that he had a girl friend who worked in a cantina in Lancha Plana on the Mokelumne River.

Instead of taking the usual precaution of disguising himself on his forays into the cities, Joaquin wore disguises in the countryside, where he and his band committed their crimes. Thus he was able to roam about the cities almost at will without fear of being recognized.

*Wells Fargo*

During the 1850s, Wells Fargo's records show shipments amounting to $5 million in gold from Mok Hill. Wells Fargo was only one of several stage companies, though, so this figure represents at best a fraction of the wealth unearthed here. Besides, most of the gold never reached the banks in the big cities. Instead, it was hoarded by its owners and then taken back east by them when they returned home.

It is true that most miners never got rich. It is also true that a good many of them got as much money as they needed to buy a farm back home, say, or start a business. The large fortunes were made by the storekeepers who sold supplies to the miners at grossly inflated prices. Nevertheless, it is estimated that the average daily wage of a miner in 1849 was $20 a day. By comparison, a day laborer might have earned a dollar a day anywhere else in the country. You can see how a reasonably frugal man could save a large sum of money in a short time.

*Odd Fellows Hall*

In 1854 Mok Hill was devastated by fires. The distinctive stone buildings here all date from after this fire. The Odd Fellows Hall was built after the fire, but the third story was not added until much later.

The center of early life in the mining towns was the hotel. Every newcomer had to stay there, and it was there that he picked up pointers on how and where to find gold. One of the earliest hotels in Mokelumne Hill was the

*Union Hotel*

Union. It was an American hotel, had three stories, and

Skyscraper at Mok.

could handle 75 men at one time. The early hotels did not
have individual rooms as a rule. Instead their clients were
housed in large dormitories, perhaps with blankets thrown
over ropes to provide a little privacy. Such places were
havens for the fierce sanguinary flea, the bedbug and body
lice.

The French hotel was the Hotel Leger, and there were *Hotel Leger*
probably others for Chileños, Mexicans, and so on.

Once they had moved to permanent quarters, the miners
kept house with the normal assiduity of bachelors when
there are no women around: abominably. They seldom
washed themselves and never shaved or cut their hair. It
was a point of honor to have an unwashed shirt—washing
clothes was a waste of time and water. It is hardly any

wonder that many of these miners, the cream of America's youth, were broken men, malnourished and disease-ridden, by the time they left the mines for home.

The placers were fabulously rich in the area of the Hill, but they began to give out about 1860. In 1861, a special
*San Andreas*    election moved the county seat to San Andreas, which had a more central location in the county. A few lode mines were opened in the area of Mok Hill, but these never amounted to much—only two, the Quaker Hill and the Boston, ever yielded as much as a million dollars—and time began to take a detour around the Hill.

Today, the Highway 49 bypass may tempt you to take a detour around the Hill, too, but don't yield to the temptation. Mok Hill still has several old buildings and a distinctive old-time atmosphere, so that taking the short side trip off the main highway is like taking a step backward in time.

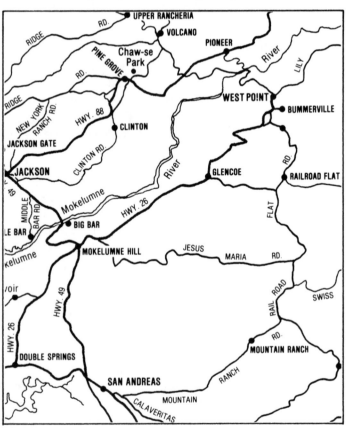

**Side trip from Mokelumne Hill: Highway 26 to West Point and Carson Pass.** Highway 26 is one of the least traveled mountain highways, which means that there are plenty of places left to be discovered along it. It passes through Happy Valley, where the French trappers had their trading post at the foot of French Hill (on the left). Both of these places had large placer deposits, as did Rich Gulch, another ghost town along the route.

*Happy Valley*

*French Hill*

After climbing through the forested hills, Highway 26 arrives in the vicinity of the East Belt lode mines. Glencoe was a center of mining activities in the 1890s. There has been some development along the highway recently, especially to the east of West Point near the National Forest.

*Glencoe*

West Point also has some agricultural industries, including ranching and walnut-growing. Bummerville is another town with a long history nearby. In the vicinity of West Point, the only actively producing gold mine in the Golden Hills is being developed by a Canadian company. The Blazing Star Mine has been capitalized at $2 million, and core samples show untapped veins of ore worth $16 a ton, a figure which should make the venture profitable. Tungsten has been discovered as well and will be mined in conjunction with the gold.

*West Point*

*Bummerville*

*Blazing Star Mine*

There are a number of other mines in the Golden Hills which could still be producing if it weren't for American business regulations requiring a public gold mine enterprise to be capitalized at a minimum of $5 million. Like many government regulations, this one was well-intentioned but has misfired. It was supposed to protect investors by assuring that mining companies had sufficient funds to develop their interests, but its effect has been to prevent the exploitation of dozens of small mines whose possible production could not justify such large expenditure.

There is little doubt that gold mining could again become an important industry in California if the price of gold were stabilized at its present level. However, the price is so speculative at the moment that no company could be formed with any long range objectives.

After West Point, Highway 26 winds down to the Mokelumne River and connects with Highway 88, the Carson Pass highway at Pioneer.

*Pioneer*

*Railroad Flat*

The East Belt mining towns are connected by Railroad Flat Road. Railroad Flat was named humorously, since its only railroad consisted of a short length of track between a mine and a mill along which a single ore car ran.

*Mountain Ranch*

One of the more interesting towns is Mountain Ranch, once named El Dorado. At first these were two separate placer mining camps, and there were others in the immediate vicinity, including one named Chee Chee Flat. The buildings in Mountain Ranch are typical of gold rush archi-

*Domenghini Store*

tecture, but here they are still being used. The Domenghini Store was built as a saloon in the 1850s and has been used continuously since that time. The Domenghini family has operated a general store in it since 1901. Mountain Ranch was an early tourist center as well as a mining town. Its attractions were San Antonio Falls near Sheep Ranch and

*Mountain Ranch Hotel*

the cave at Cave City. The Mountain Ranch Hotel is a well-preserved example of a Victorian hotel, but it is no longer in use.

*Cave City*

The cave is still at Cave City, of course. Don't rush down to see it, though, for it has suffered the fate of so many natural wonders: too many tourists have destroyed its beauty. When souvenir hunters could no longer remove anything from its walls, they amused themselves by throwing rocks at the formations on the ceiling.

## Highway 49—Mokelumne Hill to Angels Camp

*Chile Gulch*

About a mile south of Mok Hill, Highway 49 passes through Chile Gulch, the site of the Chile War. The next point of interest is the town of San Andreas, the county seat of Calaveras County. Here roads converge from all directions, including Highway 12 from Valley Springs and Jenny Lind, Mountain Ranch Road from Mountain Ranch and Sheep Ranch, and Murray Creek Road, which leads to Quiggs Mountain Lookout and the back country.

*San Andreas*

San Andreas is a fragmented town, spread out over a large area and divided into several distinct parts. From a city planning point of view, it seems to be getting ready for a population explosion. The old downtown area is separate from the rest of the town and no longer has a

*Black Bart Inn*

commercial role to play except for tourists. The Black Bart

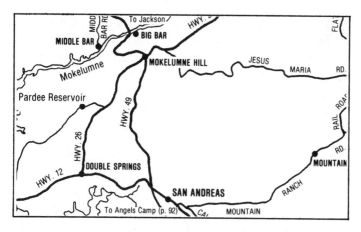

Inn is there. Directly across the street from it are two large brick buildings which are being renovated for use as a museum. When it is completed, it will be the largest museum in the Golden Hills.

Highway 49 is lined with businesses for miles, while the beautiful large homes on the hillside above it are all provided with ample space to provide an unobscured view of the valley below. The county courthouse and office buildings are located on Mountain Ranch Road at some distance from the main highway.

Gold was first discovered in the vicinity by the Mexicans, a fact which might have been deduced from the town's Spanish name. The Americans did not arrive for awhile in large numbers, because the diggings were meager and there was no convenient source of water. The Mexicans built a church and named it San Andrés after the patron saint of Spain. The present spelling is an American corruption.

In the early 1850s there were between 1,000 and 1,500 miners here working in the gullies and washes. In 1854 it was discovered that there were extensive placer deposits 150 feet below the surface. Overnight San Andreas became a boom town. The Table Mountain Water Company was formed to solve the problem of lack of water. The company built a series of ditches, flumes, and tunnels to bring water from 50 miles away, out of San Antonio Creek.

The only building of any size in the town before that time was the Bella Union, a large frame hotel. Built in

*Bella Union Hotel*

*Odd Fellows Hall*

1851, it served the town as saloon, gambling casino, meeting hall and courthouse. One of the first buildings constructed after the big strike was the Odd Fellows Hall. It was the only structure to survive the fire of 1858.

The town prospered, gathering citizens from the surrounding camps, and in 1861 it was chosen the new county seat. The records didn't reach the town from Mok Hill until 1866.

In 1883, the San Andreas jail had its most famous inmate, Black Bart. He stayed here while awaiting trial at the old courthouse and before being transferred to San Quentin.

An example of the hardships endured by the people who stayed in the Golden Hills after the gold rush was the lack of water. The miners, as we have seen, built elaborate canal systems, but when the gold was gone the residents no longer could afford to keep the ditches in repair. The problem was solved in San Andreas by the construction of numerous windmills to raise the water from deep wells. Today most of the old ditches have been repaired and currently operate under the aegis of P.G. & E.

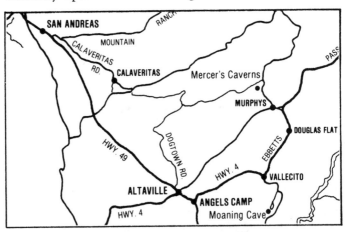

**Side trip from San Andreas:** The Calaveritas Road leads to the right from Mountain Ranch Road near the Government Center. This is a pleasant road, little used and a bit bumpy. Despite the inconvenience of driving on the smaller roads in comparison with the smooth and fast travel on the state highways, every visitor to the Golden Hills should go on at least one expedition into the interior. The highways cut a wide swath through the countryside and put a sometimes considerable distance between it and the traveler. High speed travel makes it easy to miss the delicate wildflowers, the abundant but inconspicuous wildlife, and the beautiful vistas that are so common in the foothills.

The road to Calaveritas will not take you far from the main road, but it will take you into another era. The road itself may be 75 years old, but much of the countryside has remained unchanged far longer than that. This was the old main highway between San Andreas and Angels Camp, for it passes through several old mining towns along the way.

*Calaveritas*

Do not expect too much from a ghost town and you will never be disappointed. Calaveritas still has a few old stone buildings, but the towns of Brandy Flat, San Antone and Dogtown have vanished with scarcely a trace. The road hits all the hills that the modern highway misses and crosses creeks—Calaveritas, San Antonio, Indian and San Domingo—that may be overlooked by a car speeding along Highway 49.

The Dogtown Road from Calaveritas passes leisurely through the countryside. Sometimes, when it arrives at a stream which shows signs of having been mined (with piles of tailings on both sides of the creek), it is fun to stop for awhile, look at the countryside and wonder where the town might have been, what its name was, what kind of men lived there—were they Mexicans, Americans, or Germans? If you're perceptive, you may find the foundation of a house overgrown with weeds, or some other remnant of the days of '49.

Highway 49 passes the Calaveras Cement Company, a division of Flintkote, about a mile south of town. This site was chosen for the plant in 1926 after Southern Pacific agreed to run a spur line here from Valley Springs. The plant has been the town's major industry ever since. The quarry, which can be seen from the road, is no longer in use, although the company has not tried to reclaim the land. The present source of gravel is a quarry on the Camp Nine Road near Vallecito. There, gravel is mixed with water to form a slurry and is pumped through a seven-inch steel pipe for 18 miles to the plant.

*Calaveras Cement Company*

*Altaville*     The next town is Altaville, or "High-town," standing on a ridge overlooking the hills and valleys to the east. This place was known as Forks-in-the-Road at first, because the road to Murphys separated from the road to Angels at this point. When a few more people arrived and set up camp here, it was known as Winterton and Cherokee Flat. It wasn't until 1857 that its residents decided it needed an official name, at which time Altaville was decided upon.

During the 1850s, Altaville was a way station for freight wagons going to Murphy's Diggings. Its first industry was *Demorest Iron* the Demorest Iron Foundry, which was established to *Foundry* manufacture mining equipment for the lode mines at Angels Camp and Carson Hill. The foundry is still operating today.

There are quite a few old vehicles around town, as befits a transport center. Some are located in a private shopping center at the north end of town, and others have been placed on display at the museum on the east side of the highway.

One of the most unusual of these vehicles is an old logging engine which used to haul "trains" of timber carts along the toll road from the hills for use in the mines. The huge iron wheels had wooden "tires" on them as the engine rolled down the road under a full head of steam. These ungainly vehicles were the true forerunners of the automobile, since they ran on a road which could be used by other forms of transport instead of on a track.

The toll road between Murphy's Diggings and Altaville was built in 1865. It was six miles long and 18 feet wide. In 1971 Altaville was officially annexed to Angels Camp.

*Angels Camp*     Perhaps the most famous town in the Golden Hills is Angels Camp. But its renown rests on something that may never have happened and its publicist was a man who spent no longer than a few days in the region. The symbol of Angels Camp is a bullfrog, certainly not one its residents would have chosen themselves.

The area around Angels was first settled in 1849. A man by the name of Angel had a trading post there, but little is known about him, not even his given name. Some sources refer to him as George Angel, while others identify him as the Henry P. Angel who owned the Cave City cave and operated a hotel there.

The placer gold deposits at Angels Camp were never very productive, and they soon gave out altogether. The town owed its early prosperity entirely to the rich deposits of gold in the quartz veins running underneath it. One of the earliest mines was the Invincible, later called the Utica. Utica reservoir in Alpine County was built to supply this mine with water power to drive its mill.

*Utica Mine*

Angels Camp.

From 1860 to 1866 the Utica was owned and operated by James P. Fair, the Silver King of Virginia City. The ground above the mine is now a park. The depression of the ground was caused by a cave-in in 1889 which killed 17 men. So extensive was the damage to the mine that the last body was not recovered for 15 years.

During the 1890s, many mines were expanded by consolidation with other adjoining properties, and the Utica was no exception. Although, the Utica Consolidated had 180 stamps operating in four mills. In three years, 1893–1895, four million dollars worth of gold were processed in these mills. By the time the last mine closed down in 1916, $30 million had been taken from the ground beneath Angels Camp.

Angels was notable for its large Oriental population during the 1870s. Between an eighth and a quarter of the population was then Chinese. Two brick buildings are all that remain of old Chinatown.

The large Catholic Church, St. Patrick's, was built in 1902. At that time the population of the town was about 4,000.

After the first World War, the mines never reopened and many of the miners who had left to serve in the army never returned to the town. Angels Camp was very calm and peaceful when the first paved street was put in in 1928. Almost as a joke, someone suggested they hold a jumping frog contest to celebrate the event.

*Jumping Frog Contest*

Up to this time the only jumping frog contest ever held in Angels Camp was the one described by Mark Twain in the story that first won him national attention. According to the story, Twain had been staying on Jackass Hill across the Stanislaus from Angels with his friends the Gillis brothers. He tried his hand at prospecting around Angels without success, but it was there that he heard an old prospector tell a story in the Angels Camp Hotel, a story which became his own personal gold mine.

Upon returning to San Francisco, Twain got a job writing for the *Californian*, whose editor was another young writer by the name of Bret Harte. The two got to talking to each other, telling each other their experiences in the West, and Twain happened to mention that he had just come from the mines. The people there, he claimed, were the laziest men on the face of the earth; they did nothing all day but sit around the stove in the saloon, spit, and swap lies. Bret Harte suggested that Twain recount one of these yarns for the paper, and that was how "The Celebrated Jumping Frog of Calaveras County" was born.

The story was published first in a New York journal and enjoyed immense popularity. It concerns a contest between two athletic frogs and a wager on which of the two could jump the farther. The contest was held, but the frog who lost had been loaded up with quail shot—which might have been a good argument for government regulation of the sport.

The first real frog jump was called the Jumping Frog Jubilee. The day it was held there was a traffic jam on Angel Camp's one paved street. Since the event was so successful, the promoters decided to try it again the next year, and every year since.

The Frog Jump has recently been combined with the County Fair. Both are held at the fairgrounds, called Frogtown, on the third weekend in May. A few years ago the event showed signs of getting out of control: about 75,000 people attended the three-day happening, including a number of motorcycle clubs, and the attendant publicity was so bad that the Frog Jump was almost discontinued. Since that time, however, attendance has leveled off at about 30,000, and the event has become fun again.

One of the other attractions of fair week is the traditional miners' wash, in which local groups get together clotheslines hung with outlandish articles of clothing, including unmentionables. These are then strung across the main street of town and prizes are awarded to the best ones.

Angels Camp still retains an old-time atmosphere from the time when small towns were the backbone of American life, when every town had a main street, a movie theater, and a church. In addition, Angels has the Angels Camp Hotel, where Mark Twain allegedly first heard the story of the Jumping Frog. Located on the main street, it has an historic marker in front of it with a bronze frog perched on top of the marker. It is a monument to the history of fiction and to the fiction of history.

*Angels Camp Hotel*

**Side trip from Angels Camp: Highway 49—Frogtown, Carson Hill and Stevenot Bridge.** Frogtown, not far south of the town of Angels Camp, has a short landing strip for light planes. Along the road on the way to Carson Hill you can still see a few traces of the Sierra Railroad's spur line, now discontinued. An outstanding example of gold rush architecture is the Romaggi Fandango Hall, once the center of community life for Albany Flat. Albany Flat is no more, but the Romaggi building remains, one of the largest early stone buildings and one of the best preserved.

*Frogtown*

*Romaggi Fandango Hall*

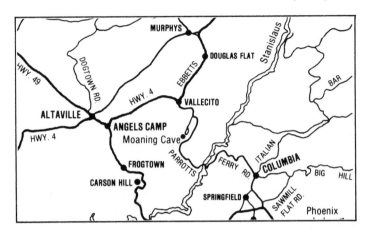

**Carson Hill**    The town of Carson Hill was once synonymous with the
Morgan Mine. The rest stop in the town has an excellent
view of the glory hole from which $26 million in gold was
taken. This was another of the concerns owned by James
Fair, the ubiquitous mining tycoon of the 1860s. In 1854 the
largest chispa ever found in the U.S. was thrown down by
an explosion. It was a 214-pound gold and quartz mass that
sold for $40,000. The gold in it weighed 195 pounds and
would be worth somewhere in the neighborhood of $600,000
today.

**Morgan Mine**    One of the reasons that the Morgan produced so much
gold was that the geographic location of the gold-bearing
quartz vein made recovery inexpensive. The vein was very
wide and ran through the entire hill. Starting at the top of
the hill, the engineers cut a mine shaft straight down to a
point that was only slightly below the level of the ground at
the bottom of the hill. A nearly level tunnel was constructed to this point so that ore cars could be brought to the
bottom of the shaft. Then, in order to recover the ore, the
miners blasted chunks off the sides of the shaft. The chunks
fell to the bottom of the hole where they could be recovered easily, and the process began again. After a minimum of time and labor spent in building long shafts and
adits, a large quantity of ore could be taken to the mill for
processing.

This method of mining eventually caused the whole top
of the hill to collapse, making an enormous crater called a
glory hole.

Glory hole at Carson Hill.

The gold in the Morgan mine occurred in pockets of extremely valuable ore—a characteristic of this section of the Golden Hills. One of the largest pockets ever discovered was thrown down from a section of earth 8′ x 8′ x 16′ in which was $3 million worth of gold. At today's prices the figure would be at least ten times that high.

The Morgan mine closed down before the first World War, but it was purchased by W. J. Loring and his syndicate in 1920 for $400,000. For the succeeding five years it repaid its owners a million dollars annually, showing that it is indeed possible to get rich with gold mining stock. It is also possible to get poor that way.

In 1975 the Carson Hill Consolidated properties were purchased with a view toward reopening them. However, only prospecting has been done at this time.

The small ore car at the Carson Hill rest stop is a monument to Archie Stevenot, whose name is also borne by the large bridge across the Stanislaus farther down the road.

*Archie Stevenot*

Stevenot was one of those rare individuals who can provide the rest of us with an example. He was a mining engineer. In fact, his whole family were mining people. His father was the superintendent at the Morgan Mine (a position Stevenot later held), and his uncle, Emil K. Stevenot, was the Borax King of San Francisco.

Archie had already lived a full life when he retired from mining and started his second career. He became a promoter for the Mother Lode. He worked with historical societies, the Golden Chain council, and government agencies to improve roads and help make tourism an industry which could take the place of mining in the Golden Hills. He worked at his second career for 15 years, and at the time of his death in the early '60s he was known far and wide as Mr. Mother Lode.

Logging trucks crossing Stevenot Bridge.

*Archie Stevenot Bridge*

The bridge that bears his name commands a breathtaking view of the Stanislaus River canyon. Carson Hill is also clearly visible, although a great deal of money has been spent on landscaping to conceal the scars of fifty years of mining. The bridge is 440 feet high. When the lake is filled, the water will back up to within 20 feet of the bridge at maximum flood.

*Melones*

From the turnout at the north end of the bridge, you can see Jackass Hill across the canyon. You cannot see the site of Melones, the gold rush town which gave its name to the lake which buried it under 400 feet of water. James Carson, who gave his name to the hill, was the first American to mine in this area in 1848. The Mexicans were more numerous, however, and they gave the town its name: they called it Melones because coarse gold nuggets found here were as big as melon seeds.

Such riches soon attracted the attention of the American miners, who came in great numbers. Some reports say as many as 5,000 miners were digging in the stream bed at the same time. The Americans thought the town needed another name, one which better described the deplorable conditions prevailing in the camp. After extensive deliberation, they decided to call it Slumgullion.

Later, when the town became a resort, the name was changed back again. At that time, too, someone decided that Melones must have been the site of Bret Harte's famous story, "The Luck of Roaring Camp." Previously the honor had been claimed for Columbia, and now that Melones has been submerged a new resort in Amador County has put in a bid for the name.

Actually, Bret Harte probably did pass through Melones—once—when Robinson's Ferry was operating here.

One of the benefits of the Melones project has been the construction of two fine bridges, one here and the other at Parrotts Ferry. This one has cut 20 minutes off the driving time between Sonora and Angels Camp. There will be recreational facilities at both ends of the bridge when the project is completed.

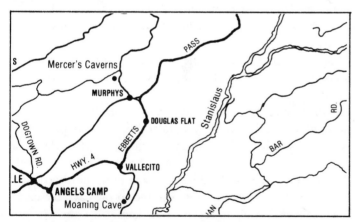

## Highway 4—Angels Camp to Ebbetts Pass

Highway 4 no longer follows the old toll road, although that road was used for more than a century. The old road was closer to the creek and followed the undulations of the land more closely.

*Vallecito*

The first town east of Angels is Vallecito. The town was first known as Murphys Diggin's and then as Murphys Old Diggin's, for the Murphy brothers set up their store here before moving it to the more promising east belt location. Large deposits of gold were not discovered here until 1852. After that, there were a number of towns near here, including Wade's Flat, Humbug Hill and Coyote Creek.

*Dinkelspiel Store*

The Dinkelspiel Store still stands as a reminder of the old days. A fire closed it for two years in 1975, but it is now open for business once more. The other attraction of the town is an old bell hanging on a monument. If this old bell could speak, what tales it could tell—but none, we imagine, as elaborate and fanciful as the stories men have told about the bell itself!

In the first years of the gold rush, there were few services provided to the miners by the government or anyone else. Each man had to be willing to serve on a posse and in a volunteer fire brigade, and do his own cooking and sewing as well. Self-reliance was the order of the day, so much so that when a man was killed he was generally considered to be at fault for not being able to defend himself and his murderer was nearly always acquitted. On the other hand, the crime of theft was severely dealt with, sometimes summarily, with a rope and the branch of a handy tree.

*Moaning Cave*

The road south from Vallecito leads past Moaning Cave, a commercial cave and one of the first to be discovered. Moaning Cave's formations have not suffered damage over the years, largely because there is only one huge room and most of the stalagmites and stalactites are out of reach.

The descent to the bottom of the cave is made by a circular staircase. When this staircase was first installed, the moaning sounds made by the cave myteriously ceased, but recent experiments have restored to the cave the eerie sounds from which it received its name.

*Parrotts Ferry*

Farther down the road you will pass the site of Parrots Ferry. Early ferries were simple affairs, generally rafts connected to either shore by ropes. The method of propulsion varied, but often consisted of a draft animal on either shore. Although large sums of money could be raised when the water was high, business was seasonal, as the rivers were frequently fordable during the dry seasons.

The next town along the Ebbetts Pass Highway is Douglas Flat. This small town retains its antique flavor, but you must leave the highway to see it. Gold was discovered under Table Mountain here for the first time in 1855. The discovery attracted miners from all over the Golden Hills to the towns at the foot of Table Mountain: Douglas Flat, Vallecito, Shaws Flat. *Douglas Flat*

*Table Mountain*

The peaceful, tree-lined streets of Murphys will be attractive to any visitor. These are cottonwoods, whereas in more recent times the trees most frequently planted are sycamores. The town takes its name from two early residents, the Murphy brothers, John and Daniel, who set up a trading post here in 1848. They were an enterprising pair of Irishmen who were partners with Charles Weber in the short-lived Stockton Mining Company. Ellen Murphy, their sister, married Weber, and became mistress of the Campo de los Franceses estate.

The Murphy family had crossed the Sierra shortly after the Donner party in 1844, following much the same route as their ill-fated predecessors. By the time gold had been discovered, they were already well-established in the Golden Hills, and they shrewdly decided to sell provisions to the miners instead of trying to find gold themselves. *Murphys*

After only a year in business, both men had made their fortunes. John left for San Jose, where he later became mayor. Daniel went into cattle ranching with enormous tracts of grazing land in California, Nevada and Mexico.

Murphys Diggin's was the richest placer camp in Calaveras County. By 1850 it boasted 1,200 miners working in the gullies and ravines around the town; soon there were thousands. It was a tent town with no permanent structures at first. Each ethnic minority had its own settlement apart from the others. Stoughtenburgh was the German camp, while the French named their settlement Algiers. Other communities in the neighborhood were Owlsburg, Brownsville and French Camp. *Murphys Diggin's*

Jim Carson, the discoverer of Carson Hill, visited Murphys and described it in a book. It was the first book

A pioneer church at Murphys.

published in Stockton and the first real tour guide of the Golden Hills. He estimated the population at 3,000 in the early '50s and called Murphys Diggin's the Mountain Queen.

*Oro Plata Mine*

There were lode mines around the town. Among these was the Oro Plata mine, which was already being worked with crude arrastras in the '50s and had a mill in operation by 1861.

*Big Trees of Calaveras*

But gold was not the only treasure Murphys could rely on. The Big Trees of Calaveras were discovered around

1850 and soon drew visitors from all over the world. For awhile these trees were the only known grove of giant Sequoias.

James L. Sperry operated a stage line to the grove as well as two hotels, one in Murphys (now the Murphys Hotel) and one at the grove. Sperry's home is one of the town's charming old houses. Across from his hotel, which has been added to in recent years, is the Old Timers Museum, one of the better private museums. It is housed in an old building that looks as if it was intended to be a fortress rather than a store: the walls are solid rock and windowless, and there is a water supply inside the building. The museum is owned by Dr. R. Coke Wood, a specialist in the history of Calaveras County who was designated "Mr. California" by the State Legislature in 1969.

*Old Timers Museum*

The contents of the museum include various curios and memorabilia. There is an old bar and a well. In addition, there is a bookstore with a large variety of guide books and historical reprints.

The most startling object is a wooden grave marker purported to be that of "Mrs. Joaquin Murietta." The fact that it was not discovered until 1956 "during an earthquake" makes its authenticity suspect, but two other points make it doubtful as well.

*Mrs. Joaquin Murietta*

In the first place, the practice of giving the husband's name rather than the wife's name is almost unheard of. By doing this, the author of the marker has neatly sidestepped one of the inconsistencies in the Joaquin legend, namely that the early writers disagreed on his wife's and his girl friend's names.

Even more damaging is the spelling of the name Murrieta, in which the grave marker follows the early writers. The name comes from the Spanish word *murria*, which means sadness or melancholy, especially the sadness following the death of a loved one. Since all the Joaquin stories picture the outlaw as avenging the death of someone, his surname may have been something completely different.

We should not deduce from the above rather scholarly observation that Joaquin Murrieta was a purely legendary figure, or that he did not live in the town of Murphys. On the contrary, the best story, the one written by John Rollin

Ridge, relates that many of the bandit's crimes were committed in the Murphys area. Here Joaquin was publicly flogged and forced to watch a friend hanged for the alleged theft of a horse. This incident in 1851 started his criminal career, which was to last for three years. His first actions were to track down and murder all the members of the lynch mob that had hanged his friend.

Joaquin soon spread out his base of operations to include most of the foothills on the east side of the San Joaquin Valley. Towns where his exploits are recounted include Fiddletown, Lancha Plana, Mokelumne Hill, Sawmill Flat, Murphys, Columbia, Hornitos, and Coalinga. This last, in Fresno County on the west side of the valley, is where he had a retreat, a secret hide-out, if you wish. It was to this hide-out that Harry Love tracked the band of outlaws in 1854 with his posse of California Rangers. Love caught up with the Mexicans as they sat around a bonfire, and opened fire. He put Joaquin's head into a glass jar and pickled it with alcohol in order to collect the bounty for his capture. The head of Joaquin Murrieta was displayed all over the state for 50 years before it was lost in San Francisco during the 1906 earthquake.

*Murphys Elementary School*

Other buildings of interest in Murphys are the Murphys Elementary School, known to the early residents as Pine Grove College. Since the closest high school was in San Francisco, the locals felt it was only fair that once they graduated here they could say they had been to college. The schoolhouse is one of the prettiest around, built in 1860.

*St. Patrick's Church*

The Catholic church, St. Patrick's, was built in 1858 by Father James Motter, whose church-building activities also gave places of worship to San Andreas, Angels, Campo Seco, and Albany Flat.

*Mercer's Caverns*

**Side trip from Murphys:** Mercer's Caverns are about one mile north of the town along a typical mountain road, narrow, winding, and picturesque. The entrance fee is a little high ($2.25 for an adult), but a visit to the caves is well worth it. The caves were discovered by Walter Mercer in 1885. There are several rooms containing an unusual variety of crystalline formations. Near the bottom of the caves is a

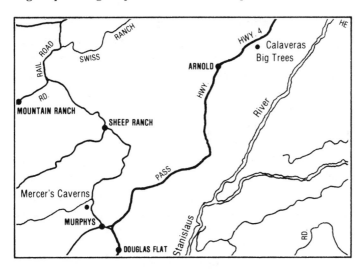

deposit of ergotite, a rare mineral. There is also an helic-
tite, which is like a stalactite except that instead of hanging
straight down it grows in the shape of a corkscrew.

The road to Mercer's Caverns continues on to Sheep     *Sheep Ranch*
Ranch, an isolated mountain town which owes its existence
to the Sheep Ranch Mine, now closed. The mine was
owned by George Hearst's mining syndicate in 1875, but his
son, William Randolph, always stayed at home in San
Francisco when his father visited his property. Willie
probably never visited Sheep Ranch.

The single attractive building in the town, near the ruins
of the mine, is the Sheep Ranch Hotel, an exquisite Vic-    *Sheep Ranch*
torian structure. Unfortunately, it is not open to the public.  *Hotel*

After passing by Murphys, Highway 4 begins to climb
into the National Forest. The yellow or ponderosa pines
grow larger and the incense cedars cluster ever more
thickly together at the side of the road. Under the trees
new vacation homes have been built in subdivisions like
Forest Meadows, Timber Trails, Pinebrook, Lakemont
Pines, and more.

This region used to be famous for its apple trees. The
only apple ranch left along the highway is located at Darby    *Darby Knob*
Knob, where apples, apple butter, jam, and cider are still
offered to the public.

Arnold used to be an apple ranch. Over a thousand trees    *Arnold*
grew here. Today it is a thriving resort town and a center

for the recreational opportunities offered by Stanislaus National Forest on the slopes of the snow-capped Sierra. A number of new shops have been opened here, catering to the needs of vacationers and residents alike.

Still one of the major attractions of Ebbetts Pass Highway is Calaveras Big Trees State Park. These unique giants grow only on the western slope of the Sierra. There are only a handful of young trees in this grove; most are over 500 years old. The incense cedar, a fast-growing tree, resembles the Big Tree in its shaggy red bark and its scale-like leaves. Many travelers confuse them, but while there are thousands of cedars along the highway, there are only about a hundred Big Trees in the North Grove.

*Calaveras Big Trees State Park*

Another distinctive tree that grows here is the mountain yew. It is a small, straight evergreen that bears a resemblance to a coast redwood. The sugar pine also grows in the grove. These pines are the most valuable lumber product in the Sierra. Their fine-grained, durable wood has been harvested since the pioneers used it for shake shingles. As a consequence of its value, sugar pines have become rare, especially of the size and quality that you will see in this grove. Some of them are over 200 feet tall, but they are dwarfed by the giant sequoias.

The park is famous for its flowering dogwoods, which put on a pretty floral display in the spring. In the fall, their yellow leaves add a stroke of color to the brilliant natural canvas.

The earliest visitors to these groves carried back the news of the monster trees to the outside world, but their stories were too incredible to be believed. Some of the trees were cut down merely to display them elsewhere as a business enterprise. The Mother of the Forest was destroyed for this reason in 1855. Its bark was stripped off to a height of 106 feet, and since the bark contains the vascular system of the tree, as well as protecting it from fire, the tree soon died.

The bark that had been taken from the tree was shipped to London, England, where it was displayed in the Crystal Palace until it was destroyed by fire in 1866.

The big stump at the beginning of the North Grove trail was cut down even before the other, apparently just for the fun of it. The project proved difficult, for the woodsmen's axes bounced off the tough, spongy bark. They were not deterred, but continued their efforts with auger and bit. It took them nearly three weeks to fell the tree by this method. After that, it took two and a half days to push it over. The traces left by the drills may still be seen in the fallen portion of the tree, although the stump has been polished, evidently for use as a dance floor.

Many myths were spread about the Big Trees. Exaggerated claims were made for them, that they were 500 feet tall and nearly 5,000 years old. Actually, only the tallest are more than 320 feet high, while their average age is between 800 and 1,300 years. The oldest of them may in fact be more than 4,000 years old.

*North Grove*

Among the most unusual visitors to the North Grove was a herd of camels, imported from the Amur River in Siberia by the U.S. Army in 1861. They were shipped to San Francisco and then taken overland to Nevada to protect the Nevada Silver mines during the Civil War.

A popular etching was made by a man named Vischer to commemorate the event. His numerous other scenes of California helped stimulate interest in the Golden State in the rest of the country.

*South Grove*

The North Grove is more accessible and has received thousands of visitors annually for 125 years, but the South Grove is much larger. It contains 1,300 Big Trees in a nearly virgin setting. There are campsites near both groves, but these must be reserved in advance for summer use.

Major John A. Ebbetts was the first man to survey the pass which bears his name. He was looking for a feasible railway route through the mountains in 1853. The Emigrant Road was much used during the 1850s, although it was not much more than a footpath over which foolhardy souls tried to bring oxcarts. The first wagon road from Murphys to the Big Trees was completed in 1856, and work on the Ebbetts Pass road began in 1862.

*Snowshoe Thompson*

Snowshoe Thompson was a famous and frequent user of the road, although he generally passed this way only when the road was buried under a thick blanket of snow. Thompson was a Norwegian emigrant who carried the mail on skis for 20 years, daily risking his life in the service of the Post

Office. The U.S. Government never paid him a dime for his efforts, which left him understandably upset.

Snowshoe Thompson was the most famous of the skiing mailmen in the Sierra, but not the only one. Today the mail is delivered by more efficient means, if a bit more costly. Skis have been handed over to the sportsmen along with the ski bowls of the Sierra.

*Bear Valley*

The largest and best equipped resort along Highway 4 is Bear Valley. The slopes of Mount Reba provide the perfect setting for winter fun. The resort has recently expanded to include new runs to the other side of the mountain.

The highway is closed by the snow every year not far beyond Bear Valley, but with the spring thaw a whole new playground opens up. Fishing for trout is a popular pastime, with the best results to be had in the most isolated regions. Hunting is permitted at certain times of the year depending on the quarry. Deer season is in the fall, and a surprisingly large percentage of the hunters get what they came for, but the season is getting shorter and shorter all the time.

Those who have their sights set on smaller game will find it in abundance. Quail, dove and squirrel each has its season. There are many game preserves in the lower foothills where more exotic animals are raised, fattened up and turned loose.

*Lake Alpine*

Highway 4 has many lakes. The most popular is Lake Alpine, just across the Alpine County line. The summit is in Alpine County at 8,700 feet. This fascinating county is the least populous in the state, yet has more than its share of things to see and do. It was formed in 1864, when the west had gone silver-crazy. The small deposits found here hardly justified the formation of a county, but several mining towns boomed for awhile, including the county seat, Silver Mountain City.

*Silver Mountain City*

When the silver boom fizzled, Alpine County was left with only a few hardy residents and a handful of ghost towns. Today it sits on the crest of the Sierra, a mute reminder of another era.

## Part Five:

## Highway 88—Camanche Lake to Carson Pass - Amador County

The easiest access to the Golden Hills from the heavily traveled highways and populous cities of the Central Valley is along Highway 88. This is Amador County, named for an early settler. Don Pedro Amador came to California with the Spanish military in 1771, but the county could equally well have been named for his son, Jose Maria, also a soldier. The Spanish word means "lover."

Camanche Lake is one of the more recent additions to the growing number of foothill lakes. It was completed in 1964 as a part of East Bay Water District's system of reservoirs, canals and power houses to provide water and power for the cities of Oakland and Berkeley. Highway 12 leads past the South Shore, where there is a park for picnics, camping and boating. It may be reached by turning east at Clements.

*Camanche Lake*

The north shore of the lake has also been developed, especially with suburban subdivisions, but also with public facilities. These may be reached by Camanche Parkway North, a new road.

To the north of the parkway lies the Jackson Valley. This valley was once the home of several thousands of Miwoks. It provided all their needs, as it was covered with oaks. Two salmon runs annually enriched their diet, and in times of trouble, Buena Vista Buttes provided them with a natural citadel, complete with a spring for fresh water.

*Jackson Valley*

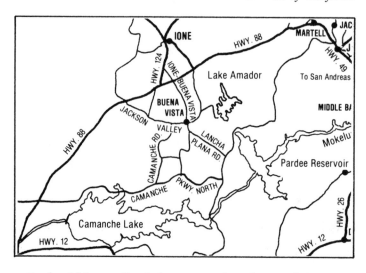

It should be realized, however, that these Indians were Miwoks, not Comanches, as the name of the reservoir might lead you to believe.

*Mokelumne*
*River Canyon*

*Lancha Plana*

Camanche Lake covered a number of historic sites in the Mokelumne River canyon. There were many early gold mining camps here, the largest of which was Lancha Plana. A lancha plana is a flat boat, which was what the early ferries looked like.

Other nearby camps were Poverty Bar, Camp O'pera, and French Bar. As usual, the various nationalities kept to themselves.

*Buena Vista*

The Jackson Valley may be traversed by the Jackson Valley Road, just past Jackson Creek on Highway 88. In the middle of the valley is the town of Buena Vista. The old stone store here is actually a relic of Lancha Plana, since it was removed from that town and brought here stone by stone. The Chinese laborers had to carry the stones seven miles, nearly all uphill.

*Buena Vista*
*Buttes*

South of the town rise the Buena Vista Buttes. A road passing between them—Camanche Road—may be reached from either Coal Mine Road or Jackson Valley Road.

*Pardee Reservoir*

Another lake in the vicinity is Pardee Reservoir, also owned by East Bay Water. Since it is a source of drinking water, no swimming or water skiing is permitted here. The dam was built by W.P.A. funds during the Great Depression. Instrumental in its construction was Grant

Miller, an Oakland mortician who was a native of Amador County.

The back road along Stony Creek leads to Jackson. Along the way is Lake Amador, a comparatively small reservoir. *Lake Amador*

The first town along Highway 88 is Ione. It was an early town, important during the gold rush for its agricultural production. Ione Valley provided watermelons, vegetables, hay and grain for the hard-working miners of Jackson and Volcano. *Ione*

The town was likely to be a stop-over for the miners on their way to the gold fields. In return for its hospitality, the newcomers gave it the uncomplimentary names of Bedbug and Freezeout. Eventually the town took the name of the valley, which was named after the heroine of Thomas Lytton Bulwer's popular novel, *The Last Days of Pompeii*.

Rancho Arroyo Seco is the tract of land to the north and west of Ione—but it wasn't always. The rancho was one of the floating grants handed out by the Californian governors when the land was part of the province of Mexico called Alta California. Rancho Arroyo Seco was bought by Andres Pico, the brother of the Mexican governor, before gold was discovered. *Rancho Arroyo Seco*

In March 1848, Pico learned he might have made a very shrewd bargain. He naturally assumed that his grant included the richest lands around. The limits of the original grant were for a parcel of ten square leagues (about 70 square miles) anywhere between the Cosumnes and the Mokelumne Rivers. The eastern boundary was given as the Sierra Nevada, and this boundary caused a great deal of trouble, as Pico contended it meant the crest of the Sierra, but the mining companies who contested his claim said that it meant the foot of the Sierra.

Pico started to cash in his property by selling tracts of it to the highest bidders. One sale concerned 5,760 acres of prime gold mining property. It was for the townships of Amador, Sutter and Jackson, and included the mining claims later to be worked as the Spring Hill, Keystone, Amador, Union, Eureka, and Badger mines. The gold produced by these mines amounted to over $100 million, while the price paid was a modest $9,000.

In the end neither this sale nor any other was allowed to go through, as the courts decided that Pico's grant did not extend as far as the gold-producing strip now known as the Mother Lode. Instead, his successors (for Pico sold his holdings before the final verdict came down) had to be content with the fertile Ione Valley. Immediately there was another rash of court cases filed by the settlers in this region, who naturally believed that they held clear title to the land by virtue of having bought it and homesteaded it.

The final court ruling came in 1862. There was no doubt about the validity of the grant, and the settlers were forced to leave their homes. A final compromise allowed them to *Muletown* keep the land in the town of Ione. The towns of Muletown and Quincy had to be abandoned. In the course of a month, *Quincy* the site of Quincy had been so thoroughly razed that no one even remembers where it was. Muletown had a happier fate, as brick from its business district was used to build up the town of Ione.

In 1876 Ione became the eastern terminus of the Galt and Ione Railroad, a spur line belonging to the Central Pacific. In 1907 a short line was completed between Ione and Martell to serve the mining and lumber interests there. The last steam engine to operate on this line, Iron Ivan, occupies a place of honor in the center of town.

*Preston School of* Another monument in Ione is the Preston School of
*Industry* Industry, often referred to as Preston Castle because of its unique architecture. It was the first reform school in the

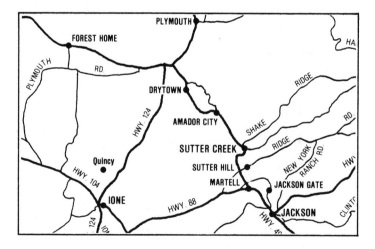

state, and remains a monument to the philosophy that youthful offenders should be educated rather than merely punished. That it was intended as a prison, too, explains its fortress-like appearance and its use of brick rather than wood as a building material.

The structure was declared unsafe under the new earthquake ordinances in 1964, but it was saved from the wrecker's ball by Ione's indignant citizenry. It is now an historical monument.

Ione holds an annual homecoming picnic and parade on the first weekend in May. The event is one of the oldest of its kind, having been held for over 125 years.

**Side trip from Ione:** Highway 104 takes you out of town to the west. About three miles outside of town a right turn on the Michigan Bar Road will take you to Carbondale, a most unusual ghost town. As the name implies, it was coal, not gold, that made men tunnel under the earth around Carbondale. Coal was the leading source of energy for the steam engine, and a few mines were opened in California in the 1860s and 1870s.

*Carbondale*

The quality of the coal mined here was not very good. Consequently, when oil was discovered in great quantities in California, the coal mines were closed. That was over fifty years ago, but there are still remnants of mine buildings and machinery in the vicinity of Carbondale.

If you continue on along the Plymouth Road, you will pass by the site of Forest Home, a gold rush settlement located on Highway 16. An old cemetery and a pile of rubble mark the place where hundreds of miners dug for gold. After passing Forest Home, you may proceed along Highway 16 to Plymouth.

*Forest Home*

*Plymouth*

After the Ione turn-off, Highway 88 continues to Martell. Here is the mill of American Lumber Products, a division of Bendix. A good view of the operations of the mill can be had from Highway 49. The plant is the largest industry in Amador County, producing lumber, plywood and fiberboard from yellow pine, sugar pine, white fir and Douglas fir. Some of the lumber milled is obtained from private holdings in the forests, while much of it is harvested from the National Forests on a sustained yield basis.

*Martell*

The opening of this plant coincided with the closing of the mines in 1941–42. The location takes advantage of the Ione Railroad.

*Jackson*

*Jackson Butte*

Highway 88 joins Highway 49 at Martell and continues down the hill southward to the town of Jackson. The grade approaching Jackson provides an excellent view of the county seat, Jackson Butte, and the valley to the east. In 1848 this valley was devoid of the traces of civilization. Where Jackson grew up there was a spring called Bottileas, or Botellas—bottles in Spanish. Legend has it that a number of bottles were found around the spring, but this seems unlikely.

Bottles were not always the disposable objects they are today. In the early days of the state, bottles of all kinds were rare. They were used and reused until the bottoms fell out. It is hardly likely that a large number of bottles would be found anywhere—except in a saloon.

In fact, there was a saloon at the spring. It belonged to Louis Tellier, the first European settler. He kept a complete stock of imported wines and liqueurs. Anyone who has ever seen a well-stocked bar can imagine how the sight would have affected the Mexicans, to whom bottles were almost unheard of.

Soon the residents decided to name their town after Colonel A. M. Jackson, who had moved here from Jacksonville on the Tuolumne River. He had been a leader in the Mexican War and many of the miners had served under him.

In 1850 Jackson had grown sufficiently to boast 100 houses and to vie with Mok Hill for the county seat. An election was held and Mok Hill won, so the county records were transferred to that place from Double Springs.

But William Smith, the first judge in the county, declared Jackson the winner. The two men who came to take the records to Jackson managed to convince Colonel Collyer, the county clerk, that he should give them up. Later Collyer accused the judge of impropriety, claiming that he had been tricked and that the election results had been falsified. Judge Smith, considering this an insult to his honor, shot and killed Collyer on the street in Jackson.

Apparently this was a bit too much for the people to take from their judge, and Smith was forced out of office.

Another election moved the county seat back to Mok Hill in 1852, but the residents of Calaveras north of the Mokelumne River decided to break away and form their own county with Jackson as the county seat.

After such hectic beginnings, the residents went back to the business of mining and building their towns. The '50s were extravagantly prosperous years in the Golden Hills. The gold deposits seemed endless, and fruits and vegetables thrived under the warm California sun.

A stage line was started in Jackson to carry mail and passengers to Sacramento in one day for a mere $20. Bull and bear fights provided amusement for the miners, and grizzly bears occasionally wandered down from the mountains to fish for salmon in the foothill streams.

A big problem for the pioneers was a lack of women. The first American woman didn't arrive in Jackson until 1850, and she was already married. Apparently the shortage was so great that many females who lived in Jackson—in the women's dormitories by the creek—decided not to limit themselves to a single man. It was not likely that these women were permitted to remain dishonest, however. California males had a habit of proposing to anyone who wore skirts, and they didn't care how their wives had earned a living.

Some women came to the camps and worked right alongside the men. One of the first women in Jackson was known as Madame Pantaloon because she wore pants and dug for gold just like the men.

Jackson must have been tolerant of foreigners, for the stories of racial friction are few. There was a large community of Jews, who were businessmen rather than miners. There were Chinese, too, who worked the gulches and creek beds long after the Americans had given up their claims and moved on to richer diggin's. Indians were numerous. They were generally treated fairly and came to the town to trade.

Jackson had a gas works during the 1850s which converted pine pitch into gas. The saloons were usually wooden buildings but they were lit by gas lights, which may have contributed to the disastrous effects of the fire of 1862 which destroyed the entire downtown area.

Later the same year the creek overflowed its banks and all the buildings next to the creek, of which the gas works was one, were washed away. After that the experiment with gas light was not continued, and the wooden pipes were used to carry water instead of gas.

*Odd Fellows Hall*

Most of the buildings in the present downtown area were built after the flood. At that time the businesses were moved farther away from the creek. The Odd Fellows Hall bears the date 1855, but that is the date of the founding of the society in Jackson.

The Odd Fellows were frequently prominent in the mining district. Their halls were often constructed of durable materials, and many of them remain standing to this day. The society had certain secret rituals, for example a secret language composed of hand signals. But its primary focus was benevolent. The Odd Fellows cared for widows and orphans and provided for the burial and funeral expenses of its members. Many of its functions were taken over by insurance companies.

The first two stories of the Odd Fellows building were built shortly after the fire, but the third story was not added until 1905. The ceilings of this story are 17½ feet high, making it the tallest three-story building in the United States.

In 1878 occurred one of those extraordinary events that startle disbelieving visitors for years to come. A cloudburst broke over the southern part of the county, and the stories told about its effects are numerous. The water was so deep in Jackson that shop owners had to swim for their lives. In Butte City, a funeral was being held just as the storm broke and the mourners rushed for cover. When they returned, they found the grave empty, and the coffin was not found until the following day. An Indian woman who had been mining in a gully apparently had fallen asleep. The gully was turned into a raging torrent by the storm, and the woman was swept away through a mining tunnel. She emerged at the other end, frightened but unharmed.

This was about the time that the mines along the Amador Strip of the Mother Lode began to be exploited to the fullest. New advances in refining made it possible to mine lower grade ores than previously. Old mines were opened up. Shafts were extended until the mines here were the deepest anywhere in the world.

There also came a time, in the 1880s, when people began to look back on the events of the gold rush as something special to be preserved in human memory. Mason's *History of Amador County* and Alley's *History of Tuolumne County* were written at about this time. Without these records the historical events of the 1850s would now be irretrievably lost.

One reaction to the feeling of importance of the past was the founding of the Native Daughters of the Golden West in Jackson in 1886. The Native Sons had been around for awhile, but this was the first women's society dedicated to the preservation of California history. Over the years the society has played an important role in preserving old buildings and setting up markers where buildings and towns had already vanished.

*Native Daughters of the Golden West*

The resumption of mining activities brought with it union activity. In 1891 the thousand members of the miners' union went on strike for higher wages. By this time the era of the individual miner striking it rich on his own had long passed. Now the companies were large and getting larger. Numerous small mines were being consolidated into a single large one.

Mine owners preferred to hire foreign emigrants rather than pay higher wages to the Americans. Federal troops were called in to protect the mines and keep them open. Yet the miners' demands were not excessive. They only wanted parity with miners working in the Nevada County gold mines: $4.00 a day for underground work, and $2.50 a day for other workers.

After the unions were broken, the mines prospered, and the towns along the Amador Strip prospered as never before. In 1916 the mines were closed by executive decree. World War I was raging in Europe, and the demand for mercury and explosives prevented their use in mining.

After the war the mines in the other counties of the Golden Hills were never reopened, but the Amador Strip mines carried on exactly as before.

*Argonaut Mine*

The worst mine catastrophe in the history of the Southern Mines occurred in 1922 when fire broke out in the Argonaut mine. The mine shaft was sealed off to smother the flames and 47 men were trapped below the surface.

Miners in the nearby Kennedy mine began working to rescue the trapped Argonauts by breaking through to them far beneath the earth. But the operation took too long, and all 47 men died. The last one scrawled the time of his probable last act of consciousness—3 a.m. August 6—along with the words, "gas too strong." The slate was found at the 4,350-foot level of the mine, already far below the level of the sea.

Before the Argonaut ceased operations in 1942 (another war had prompted another executive decree), it had been deepened to 6,142 feet. Its neighbor, the Kennedy, was 5,912 feet. At that time they were the deepest mines anywhere in the world. Both were consolidated mines. Altogether, the Argonaut had netted $25 million and the Kennedy $34 million.

Any visit to Amador County should include a walk around Jackson. The main street of the town is too narrow and crooked to have much automobile traffic, making it ideal for the pedestrian. You will have to jump up on some rather high sidewalks, however, a reminder of how deep the water used to get during heavy rainstorms.

*National Hotel*

The downtown area is well-preserved. Many of its buildings date from the 1860s and care has been taken to preserve and restore them. Besides the unique Odd Fellows Hall, there is the National Hotel, a large and distinctive establishment.

*County Museum*

The County Museum is located at the top of the hill overlooking the business district. It occupies a wood-frame house built in the 1860s by A. C. Brown for his wife and seven children. Brown served a term as County Judge in 1877. He spent some of the money he acquired during his long legal career to purchase several lots on top of the hill. These have been made into a quiet park and outdoor display area.

The Museum (hours: noon to 4:00 P.M., except Tuesday) has several maps for sale which will be of use while touring the county, as well as brochures with self-guided walking tours of the major towns.

The permanent exhibit includes many articles of nineteenth century furniture; a scale model of the argonaut mine shafts and tunnels; several other scale models with early mining themes; period firearms, Miwok basketry, and a library full of dusty tomes of the sort with which the authors are only too familiar.

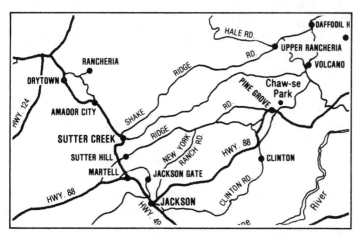

**Side trip from Jackson:** The Kennedy Mine and Tailing Wheels are located north of town on the road to Jackson Gate. Also along the road is the graveyard and St. Sava's Serbian Orthodox Church. This church, built in 1894, is the mother church of the faith in the U.S.

*Kennedy Mine and Tailing Wheels*

*St. Sava's Serbian Orthodox Church*

Only two of the four tailing wheels remain upright, although there are plans to raise a third. A pleasant park and picnic area has been developed around them. Each wheel is 58 feet tall. They were built to carry the tailings, or mine wastes, away from the Kennedy mine in accordance with an anti-debris law.

Work on the wheels began in 1914. Each was driven by a 25-horsepower electric motor. The canvas drive belt, attached to the interior rim, was 125 feet long and weighed 800 pounds. The tailings were mixed with water and allowed to flow down across the valley in a flume to the first and lowest of the four wheels. This wheel lifted the

Tailing wheel and Kennedy Mine.

slurry up to another gravity flume by means of 200 five-gallon buckets. This process was repeated until the water had surmounted the hill and flowed into the impounding reservoir. The wheels turned 14 times a minute and ran continuously for 30 years. During that time, only one fatality occurred in connection with the wheels, when a night watchman got his raincoat entangled in the works of one of the huge wheels.

While they were in operation the wheels were protected from the elements by four iron-covered buildings. The buildings were torn apart for scrap metal during World War II.

The reservoir used to impound the tailings may be seen from the summit of the higher of the two hills. The tailings themselves have a fair amount of gold in them. They were worked by dredges during the 1920s.

The Kennedy gallows and the ruins of the mill structures may also be seen across the valley from the top of the hill. The new Argonaut mine may be seen on the ridge to the left of the Kennedy. The Kennedy mill had 100 stamps, while the Argonaut had 80.

*Jackson Gate*          The road through the park continues to Jackson Gate, where the Chichizola store dates from the gold rush. The road rejoins Highway 49 at Martell.

The Jackson Gate Road is a part of the loop bicycle trail which has been posted for cycling enthusiasts and novices alike. From here, the trail follows the road and then the highway to Sutter Creek, then proceeds to Volcano along the less grueling creek route. From Volcano it runs to Pine Grove by way of Chaw-se. There is a bicycle rest stop, and after that ride you will need it. From there the route leads downhill along the Ridge Road and then to Jackson by way of the New York Ranch road. (See map, p. 121)

Another loop trail for bicycles has been used by nationally ranked riders in preparation for the 1980 Olympics. The 8.6-mile course begins at the intersection of the Ione-Buena Vista Road and the Jackson Valley Road in Buena Vista. Then it heads south along the Lancha Plana Road, across Jackson Creek and makes a right turn on the Camanche Parkway. After making another right turn on Indian Reservation Road, the loop ends at the stop sign at the Lancha Plana Road.

Bicycling in the Golden Hills can be very enjoyable. You will not see as much territory as in a car, but you will see more along the way. The quietness of the vehicle permits you to hear bird calls, the lowing of cows, and the wind whispering over the fields of grass. The tiny wildflowers can be more closely examined as you pass them along the road, and it is easier to stop and take a closer look.

It is best to stick to the back roads on your bicycle, as this will avoid the hazards so familiar to city riders: fast-moving automobiles, heavy traffic and polluted air. The roads are sometimes bumpy, and generally hilly.

*Bicycle Trail*

*Sutter Creek*

*Volcano*

*Pine Grove*

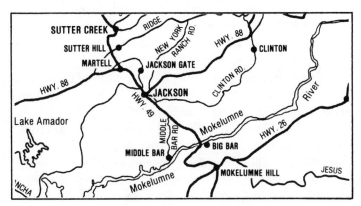

**Side trip from Jackson:** Highway 49 leads out of Jackson to the south and reaches the Mokelumne River in short order. The Middle Bar Road offers an interesting detour not far from Jackson. If you take it to the right, you will come to the Mokelumne River at Middle Bar, the site of much mining activity in the late nineteenth century.

Middle Bar attracted numerous Cornish miners from the south of England. It was only natural that these deep mine coal miners should start tunneling for gold, even as the rest of the miners were still picking nuggets out of the stream beds.

The most famous and productive mine here was a pocket mine, the Nevills. It was prospected by a pair of Germans who thought they were onto a good thing but just couldn't get along with each other. Nevills purchased the claim from them for $200 and started digging with a Mexican employee, Caesario. They worked until Nevills either got bored or just restless and headed for greener pastures in Nevada, leaving his wife with Caesario to take care of the claim.

But Mrs. Nevills never did give up. While her husband was away she made the strike, a single pocket of high-grade ore worth $200,000. When Nevills returned he discovered himself a wealthy man.

The Nevills mine was further developed by means of a large tunnel blasted through the rock. This tunnel caused the mine to be called the Mammoth.

You can still see the massive foundations which supported the gallows of the Gwynn mine. The road down to the river is an old one, steep and narrow, but there is a bridge across to Calaveras County.

Butte City was an important mining community along the road between Jackson and Mok Hill. Today there is nothing left but the Ginocchio store, built in 1856 and still well preserved in spite of its isolated location and the obvious depredations of vandals.

During the '50s Butte City had 600 houses and approximately 3,000 residents. Many of the miners were French. They early set about remaking the countryside to resemble the Mediterranean part of France, which has a similar terrain and climate. Some of the almond trees and grape stocks can still be seen.

The Americans were not fond of the Frenchmen, who kept to themselves and refused to learn English. Whenever someone addressed a Frenchman in English the only reply he got was, "Qu'est-ce qu'il dit?" ("What is he saying?"). So the Americans dubbed their Gallic counterparts "Kes-kee-dees" in retaliation.

Butte City slowly faded into the countryside. The solitary building remains because the Ginocchio family kept title to it for sentimental reasons.

The highway crosses the Mokelumne River near the site of Big Bar. This was one of the earliest gold mining camps. Nearly every one of the streams in the Golden Hills had large towns at frequent intervals along its course. A century of annual floods has erased any reminder of all but a few.

*Big Bar*

**Side trip from Jackson:** Highway 49 and the Volcano loop. Starting from Jackson, the best way to tour the county is to head north on Highway 49 past Martell. This will bring you past the County Airport to the township of Sutter. The township took its name from John Sutter, the Swiss emigrant whose ranch was the scene of the gold discovery.

*Sutter*

Sutter reportedly cut some timber nearby in 1846. Later, when the rush for gold had destroyed all the capital improvements he had made on his land, Sutter returned to this area to try his hand at mining. The gold rush that brought wealth to so many was a disaster for Sutter, who owned the land, and for Marshall, who made the actual discovery.

Sutter Creek.

*Sutter Hill*        Sutter Hill is the part of the community located at the intersection of Highway 49 with the roads to Ione and Pine Grove. Today it is best known as the site of the Italian Benevolent Society's annual picnic in June, a century-old tradition. The affair is an extravaganza of Italian cookery with parades, music and dancing added for good measure.

*Sutter Creek*        Sutter Creek is the best-preserved mining town in the Golden Hills. Many of its buildings were either constructed or remodeled in the 1890s during the lode mining boom. This gives the town a uniformity of appearance unheard of in American towns. The Victorian style includes plenty of ornamental mouldings, balconies and railings. The bright colors of the buildings are authentic.

At the south end of the town is the huge pile of tailings from the Central Eureka Mine. This was the last working gold mine; it closed down in 1958. It was the second richest mine in California, with a total production of more than $34 million. Only the North Star in Nevada City was richer.

*Central Eureka Mine*

A unique attraction of the town is Knights Foundry on the creek east of the main street. This foundry has occupied the same premises since 1873. It is the last water-powered operation in the U.S. Metal pourings are open to viewing by the public on Fridays.

*Knights Foundry*

Samuel Knight established the foundry to produce a water wheel of his own invention. He was a carpenter who had used his mechanical inventiveness to cope with the high water table at Butte City. His water wheel was turned by a high pressure nozzle, an important innovation. After the superiority of the Pelton wheel was demonstrated in 1895, Knight began manufacturing equipment for gold dredges.

Today the foundry specializes in custom-made machine parts. It receives orders from all over the world.

Amador City is the smallest incorporated city in the United States. Since the shut-down of the mines its major industry has been tourism. It has many specialty shops along its main street. Three festivals are held annually: Gold Pans and Poppies in May, Sourdough Days over the Labor Day weekend, and Calico Christmas, a crafts fair held the first weekend in December.

Amador City straddles the Mother Lode quartz vein in the middle of the Amador Strip. Its major mine was the Keystone, which produced $24 million. All told, the mines along the Amador Strip, the ten miles between Plymouth and Jackson, produced about half of the $300 million in gold taken from the southern lode mines.

*Amador City*

Amador City was larger than Sutter Creek during the gold rush, but today the situation is reversed.

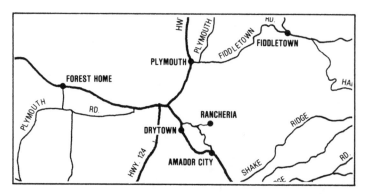

**Side trip from Amador City:** Instead of turning left at the end of the main street to continue your trip on Highway 49, turn right on Water Street in front of the Chichizola store (now housing the post office). Turn left down the alley and leave town to the north. This will take you by the Knights of Pythias Hall, the Amador City schoolhouse, and the site of the Little Amador mine (on the right end of the block).

*Knights of Pythias Hall*

You will now be traveling north on the Amador via Bunker Hill Road. The old Bunker Hill mine site is along the road. Turn right when you come to the New Chicago Road. The sites of the gold rush camps of New Chicago and New Philadelphia are along this road, as is that of the most famous ghost town in the county, Rancheria.

*Rancheria*

Rancheria is remembered, not for the wealth of gold found here, but for the Rancheria Massacre. A gang of outlaws, mostly Mexicans, killed nine people here in a single night in 1855. The people killed were eight white Americans and one Indian.

*Rancheria Massacre*

The killings were the final act in a drama of racial strife and national pride which had been going on since before the gold rush. The loss of revenues due to gold becoming scarce doubtless had something to do with the timing. Certainly one of the legitimate grievances of the Mexicans in general was the still-rankling wound left by the Foreign Miners Tax of 1851.

The tax was passed by the state legislature with the single purpose of forcing Mexicans and other foreigners off their claims. The amount of the tax, $20 a month, was high enough to accomplish this end. The Mexicans were forced off their claims, but not away from the gold fields. Some of them, like Joaquin Murrieta, turned to brigandage. Others worked the Americans' claims for them and harbored a grudge.

Many Americans were not satisfied with seeing the Mexicans impoverished. They wanted them to go back to Mexico. These men joined the Native American Party and comprised, briefly, the single largest political group in California. They were called the Know-Nothings because they refused to say anything to the press or outsiders about the goals or plans of their organization. The Rancheria Massacre suited their plans precisely.

The next morning, a vigilante group rounded up all the Mexicans they could find in and around Rancheria. They chose three men who had been seen associating with the killers and hanged them. They told thirty others to leave town immediately, and the rest of the Mexican community went with them. Once they got out of town, it was the Miwoks' turn to avenge themselves on the hated Mexicans. They harassed the retreating Hispanics, killing and wounding many of them.

Posses were soon organized to track down the killers who had headed south with all the loot they could carry. One of them, Manuel Garcia, was overtaken at Texas Bar on the Mokelumne River. The sheriff of this posse was determined that no innocent man would be punished, so he sent Garcia back to Jackson for trial. Garcia was later hanged, after the trial.

The posse continued on through Calaveras County. They caught up with the gang at Spanish Camp in a fandango house. Again the sheriff tried to take back the men uninjured and his good intentions cost him his life. There was a shootout and the sheriff and two members of the gang were killed.

Many of the other Mexicans left Amador County soon after the atrocity. Some of these returned to Mexico, and a few settled near Jenny Lind where their descendants live to this day.

It was inevitable that the Chileños suffer along with the Mexicans. They were not as numerous and they kept aloof from the Mexicans. They were lode miners and thus more

*Chilenos*

stable and peaceful than the wilder elements of the Mexican community. The Chilean quarter at Drytown was burned soon after the Rancheria murders and the Chileños were forced to leave their claims.

Not that the Americans had any justification in their treatment of the Mexicans, for they had none. The greater part of the Mexican community was composed of peons, or day laborers. They had suffered just as much at the hands of the lawless element as had the Americans. Nevertheless they were hated for their strange language and brown skin and they were expelled along with the rest.

There is a grave marker by the road at Rancheria, erected over the graves of the victims, the Dynan family, by a descendant in 1941. The town itself vanished quickly after the tragedy, for no one wished to remain in so ill-omened a place.

*Drytown*

Retrace your steps to the Bunker Hill junction. The road straight ahead leads to Drytown, the next town along the Amador Strip. It is the oldest town in the county, as there were homesteaders along Dry Creek even before gold was discovered there. Only the creek was dry—the town had 26 saloons to quench the thirst of the miners and relieve them of their pokes at the gaming tables.

Before there was much money in circulation, miners carried their dust around in little sacks. These were their pokes. The standard for business transactions was the pinch—the amount of gold dust which could be held between thumb and forefinger while the two fingers were touching. The gambling casinos and banks had scales for more accurate measurements. At the time gold was discovered, it was valued at $16 an ounce, but this soon dropped to $12 or less. It was the classic economic paradigm of a rise in the supply forcing down the demand and lowering the cost.

The ignorance of the Indians of the value of gold made their dust worth even less.

Drytown has several buildings dating from the 1850s. In the summer there are melodramas performed every Saturday night by the Claypipers, a Bay Area company. Another distinction of the town is that the first temperance society in the state founded its movement here.

Plymouth is a larger town with a more recent history. The site of the gold rush town of Pokerville is at the south end of the town, but the major industry here was lode mining and the boom period was at about the turn of the century. The principal mines were the Empire and the Pacific. These had already closed down when W. J. Loring purchased them in 1911 and began operating them together as the Plymouth Consolidated. Loring's hopes were justified, for the mine produced $7 million in five years.

Today Plymouth is an agricultural center where the memories of a mining past still linger. The county fairgrounds are located here. The fair takes place the second weekend in August, but there is a permanent display of a miniature mining town complete with boardwalk and a covered bridge. A rodeo and parade are held in Plymouth during '49er Days in October.

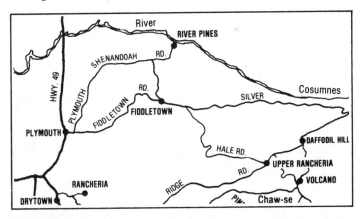

**Side trip from Plymouth:** Highway 49 leads north to Enterprise, a ghost town on the Cosumnes River. Across the river is El Dorado County with its county seat at Placerville (Hangtown) and the State Historical Park at Coloma where gold was first discovered. There is a replica of Sutter's Mill there; the original was destroyed by miners looking for gold.

**Side trip from Plymouth:** The Plymouth Shenandoah Road (E16) leads east from Plymouth through the picturesque Shenandoah Valley. Here, almost unknown, is one of the great wine-producing areas of California. There are

*Plymouth*

*Placerville*

*Coloma*

*Shenandoah Valley*

still almond groves and prune orchards alongside the vineyards, so the valley is reminiscent of places along the Mediterranean where similar crops are grown.

The principal grapes grown here are Zinfandel and Muscat. These varieties have a strong flavor which becomes overwhelming where the weather is too hot, as it is in the Central Valley. There are several wineries here which will sell wine by the case, but only the D'Agostini Winery, located at the end of the valley, offers wine tasting and a tour of the premises.

*River Pines*

The road continues by the D'Agostini property to the resort town of River Pines on the Cosumnes River. If you backtrack about a mile from D'Agostini's you will come to the Fiddletown turn-off, which will take you over the ridge into the next valley.

*Fiddletown*

Fiddletown is a small village with a long history. The principal historic attraction is the Chinese drug store, one of two rammed-earth (not adobe) buildings left in the state. Its last resident was an Oriental who died in 1965. He had kept the building in excellent repair over his long lifetime and numerous rare artifacts were found inside it after his death. It is one of the few places where the Chinese influence is visible.

The town received its name during the gold rush, it is said, from a group of Missouri fiddlers who happened to take up residence there. Years later, one of the locals became a judge whose business took him frequently to chic San Francisco hotels. The city slickers used to laugh at the name of the town, which so mortified this sober-sided citizen that he had the name changed to Oleta.

Many years after that, the townsfolk decided they liked the old name after all (no one knew why it was called Oleta) and they changed the name back to Fiddletown. Whatever it may be called, the town is a peaceful spot on the banks of Dry Creek that may make you think you are in another century—or wish you were—if only for a few moments.

The Fiddletown Road doubles back to the Shenandoah Valley Road through an entirely different sort of terrain, rough and wild instead of calm and pastoral. If you prefer, you may continue on along the Silver Lake Road through another part of the Golden Hills. The Silver Lake Road eventually connects with Highway 88, the Alpine Highway, at Dewdrop Station.

If you turn right on Hale Road two miles east of Fiddletown you will come to two other towns: one that's given up the ghost and another that's still in there pitching.

The first one is Upper Rancheria. It used to be on the hill across Rancheria Creek near the point where Hale Road makes an abrupt turn to the left. This was once a prosperous town, and several stone houses were built there. Just as quickly as it was born, it died, leaving the buildings abandoned on the hill. Then, slowly, the buildings vanished. Some were taken away brick by brick to make someone's fireplace or barbecue; others were moved in one piece to be rebuilt somewhere else.

*Upper Rancheria*

Today only a few foundations remain where Upper Rancheria once stood, but many of its buildings are still standing, having achieved a sort of life after death, in other towns.

If you should happen to make your journey into the Golden Mountains during the latter half of March or the first half of April, you will want to visit Daffodil Hill. To get there, turn left at the end of Hale Road onto Shake Ridge Road and continue on about three miles.

Daffodil Hill is a private farm whose owners have covered four acres with 200,000 daffodils. It is not a commercial venture. There is no charge for admission and no one sells souvenir postcards at the gate. Besides daffodils there are almond trees, crocuses, tulips, hyacinths, violets, and lilacs on the hill.

*Daffodil Hill*

The flowers have all been planted by the owners for their own amusement. However, what they have labored so hard to produce and spent so much money to buy belongs just as much to the visitor as to the owner.

In the same way, each nationality which came to the foothills during the gold rush brought its own plants, many of which have flourished in the hospitable climate without benefit of careful cultivation.

The French brought their almonds; the Italians brought grapes. The Spaniards brought the prickly pear cactus and the umbrella-like fig tree. The Chinese brought the Aila-

Alpine wildflowers.

canthus, the tree of heaven, with its long, snake-like branches, its brilliant yellow and orange flowers and its seed pods that rustle in the winter wind.

From Daffodil Hill, take the Rams Horn Grade Road to the right and you will arrive shortly at Volcano, the ghost town that refused to die.

*Volcano*       Volcano was one of the largest of the early settlements. One thousand persons voted here in the special election of 1855, when only Jackson had more voters. It was the first town in the gold district which emigrants came to after crossing Carson Pass, and it may have owed some surplus population to this fact.

Marble facade at Volcano.

There was gold here and plenty of it, but never the hint of a volcano. The name was suggested by the round, crater-like valley which the first miners discovered here—and then proceeded to destroy.

In contrast to other wild and wooly camps, Volcano had a cultured population. It boasted two theaters and its settlers originated the idea of a little theater group. It also had the first observatory, circulating library, law school, and debating society in California.

Many prominent citizens got their start here, including M. M. Estee, who became governor of the state. The *Amador Ledger* was started here and later moved to Jackson.

Thanks to the efforts of its citizenry the buildings in

Volcano are among the most distinctive and best preserved in the Golden Hills. They even had one, the Jug & Rose Ice Cream Parlor, moved here from Rancheria in the early 1950s. The hotel is another beautiful structure though it dates from a later period than the others. It is the fourth hotel to occupy the site since 1862. They were the National, the Eureka, the Empire, and now the St. George. Each was destroyed by fire and each time the same man rebuilt.

The Masonic and Odd Fellows orders here were the first in the state, and both have halls in the town. Not far outside the town is the Masonic Cave, where the Masons met before they had a lodge hall.

More recently the town has produced Brigadier General Harry Liversedge, the marine whose regiment placed the first American flag on Iwo Jima. His grandfather was one of the original settlers in the district, and his father had a ranch at Chaw-se.

Perhaps due to the influence of so famous a native son, Volcano erected a war memorial in Soldier's Gulch. *Soldier's Gulch*

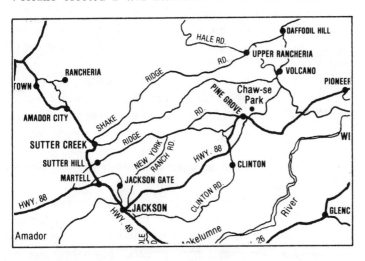

A short drive south along the Pine Grove Road from Volcano will bring you to Chaw-se Park, a name which fits more easily on maps than the previous one: Indian Grinding Rocks State Historical Park. This is a very pretty spot, as were all the places where the Miwoks congregated, for everywhere they promoted the growth of massive and stately oaks. *Chaw-se Park*

*California Oaks*

The oaks of the Golden Hills are every bit as distinctive and beautiful a natural a treasure as the Big Trees. The trees at Chaw-se are valley oaks. These are the largest of the California oaks, sometimes reaching heights of over 125 feet with broad spreading crowns and large limbs that sometimes dip down to the ground. The trunks of the older oaks reach 11 feet in diameter.

The valley oak is also known as the white oak, or roble. They once covered the entire central valley, but today their range is restricted to the foothills of the Sierra and the coast ranges. It is sometimes claimed that air pollution is harmful to them and that therefore they will soon vanish from populous areas, but this is yet to be proven.

*Valley Oak*

The valley oak is also the longest lived of our oak trees, sometimes reaching 300 years of age.

*Blue Oak*

The blue oak is a similar foothill variety, whose leaves have a more bluish tint. The black oak, the oak of Yosemite

*Black Oak*

and the upland valleys, is nearly as large as the valley oak, although its growth is more similar to the eastern oaks and its crown seldom spreads as wide. The blackness referred to is that of the trunk, but the difference between white and black oak is hardly as great as the difference between white and black.

Leaf miner tunnels on a black oak leaf.

Black oaks do not live as long as their valley cousins, for they are especially prone to rot. The branches become hollow and rotten until they fall off one by one. In the end only the trunk is left, but this may stand for many years, and provides burrows for climbing animals and birds.

The smallest oak is the scrub oak, rarely reaching above the height of a man.

*Poison Oak*

Just for the record, poison oak does not belong in the family of true oaks. It is a relative of poison ivy and has the same noxious qualities. It may resemble a small oak shoot, however, so any shrub with pointed leaves growing in groups of three should be viewed with suspicion. Residents of the Golden Hills sometimes call themselves poison-oakers, and with good reason, for the plant is abundant in shaded areas below 5,000 feet.

*Miwok Roundhouse*

The park at Chaw-se has several attractions besides the oaks. It has a Miwok roundhouse and several other struc-tures. It also has the grinding rock itself. The Miwok

Roundhouse at Chaw-se.

women (who did most of the work) gathered at this rock and others like it throughout the Sierra to grind their acorns, seeds and grains into meal. It was typical of the Miwok that no special mortars were needed for this work. Instead, the mortar was formed from the grinding of the pestle against the flat surface of the rock. The Miwoks generally chose to do things in the simplest and most direct manner with as little labor as possible.

One exception to this general rule came in the weaving of their baskets, which are so closely woven that they will hold water. The Miwoks traded these baskets with other tribes whose skills were not so far advanced.

A unique feature of the park is the Miwok cultural center. This large building has only recently been completed. Plans for its development include displays of culture and history, as well as a work area where visitors may watch native American craftsmen as they ply their trades.

*Miwok Cultural Center*

Chaw-se is level so that walking here is an undiluted pleasure. Also there is a large campground here.

Pine Grove is but a mile and a half south of Chaw-se, but at this point we should retrace our steps to Jackson before continuing any farther into the mountains.

*Pine Grove*

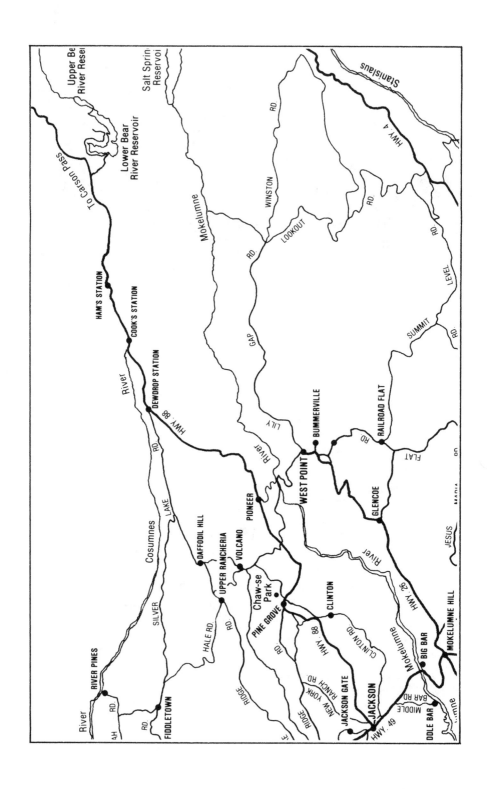

## Highway 88—Jackson to Carson Pass—
## Alpine Highway

The first town to the east of Jackson is Clinton, which may be reached from South Jackson by the Clinton Road, or from Highway 88 by the West Clinton Road. This was once a prosperous logging town, but the lumber industry passed it by long ago. Clinton Road passes close to Jackson Butte, an odd-shaped hill with an elevation of 2,300 feet.

*Clinton*

Another attraction of the area on the Mamry Road is Mount Zion State Forest, a small park next to the resort community of Pine Acres. Pine Grove is the next town along Highway 88, an old town which grew up around an inn and still retains the character of a mountain way station.

*Pine Acres*

*Pine Grove*

Pioneer is the site of a sawmill producing two-thirds of the cedar pencil stock used in the United States and exporting to countries all over the world. It was once a way station for the oxcarts making their slow and difficult passage over Carson Pass. The other stations of which some trace remains are Mace Meadows, Amador Pines, Dew Drop Station, Cooks Station, and Hams Station.

*Pioneer*

*Dewdrop Station*

In the pioneer days it was the ox, not the horse, that carried provisions over long hauls. Oxen were stronger than horses, more durable, less skittish and less expensive. Their only serious drawback was that they could travel little more than four miles a day. At that rate it took the wagon trains nine months to cross the great plains—which accounts for the fact that most of the miners were '49ers instead of '48ers.

Hollywood's western epics always feature horses in the leading roles for a very simple reason: there are no ox men left to handle the cows.

All the metal parts on the oxcarts were larger than those for horse-drawn vehicles. Rusted or broken pieces were frequently discarded along the trail and are sometimes found even today. Ox shoes are also found. Unlike horseshoes they have two parts, for oxen have cloven hoofs.

A number of new developments have joined the ranks of the older resorts along Highway 88. One of the oldest is Silver Lake, at 7,200 feet, with a history of use dating back

*Silver Lake*

well over a century. Silver Lake is one of the larger alpine lakes where the cool, rarefied air is filled with the scent of pine.

The south end of the lake was formerly part of the Plasse Ranch. Now the city of Stockton has a municipal camp there. The north end belonged to Zack Kirkwood and his large family. They also had a ranch near Jackson for winter pasturage.

*Mokelumne Wilderness*

A feature of the National Forest in this area is the Mokelumne Wilderness, jointly maintained by El Dorado and Stanislaus National Forests. Here are 50,000 acres of unspoiled forest and grasslands, with hundreds of small lakes and streams. No motors are permitted within the boundaries of a wilderness area, and you must get permission from the Forest Service before embarking on an expedition.

The stretch of highway between Pioneer and the summit is among the finest mountain highways anywhere, with several breathtaking vistas along the way. The road was once cut into two parts at Carson Spur. In order to proceed past this point, wagons had to be lifted by means of pulleys up a steep cliff. Oxen went up the same way, with a sling under their bellies.

*Kirkwood Meadows*

Kirkwood Meadows was once a part of the Kirkwood Ranch. Today it is an ultra-modern ski bowl. Work was not begun here until Highway 88 was made an all-weather highway in the early 1970s to relieve traffic congestion on Highway 50.

In 1975 NASTAR and the Far West Ski Association named Kirkwood the foremost California ski resort. The trails run from 9,827 feet at Thimble Peak down to 7,850 feet at the bottom. In addition the resort has 15 miles of cross country ski trails and condominium and chalet developments.

Since Highway 88 is open all year round, it is the newest winter route to Lake Tahoe. At any time of year it is the most scenic way to get there.

# Ghost Towns in Amador County

From *Ghost Towns of Amador*, by Valley Publishers, $3.95.

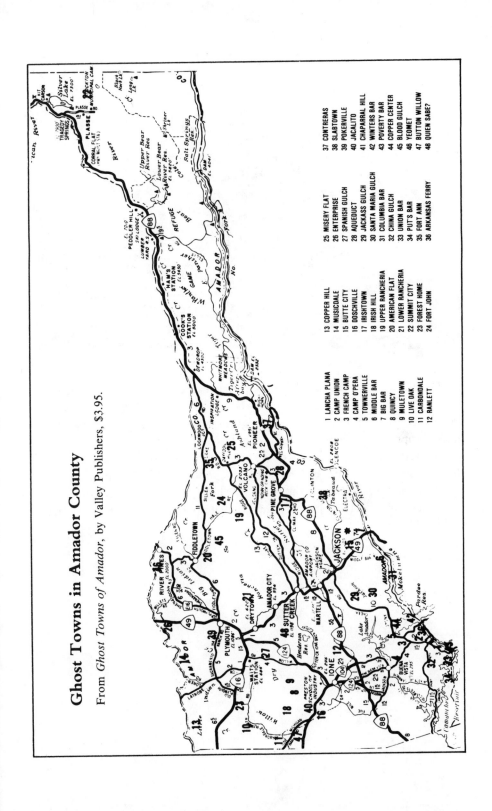

| | |
|---|---|
| 1 LANCHA PLANA | 13 COPPER HILL |
| 2 CAMP UNION | 14 MUSICDALE |
| 3 FRENCH CAMP | 15 BUTTE CITY |
| 4 CAMP OPERA | 16 DOSCHVILLE |
| 5 TOWNERVILLE | 17 IRISHTOWN |
| 6 MIDDLE BAR | 18 IRISH HILL |
| 7 BIG BAR | 19 UPPER RANCHERIA |
| 8 QUINCY | 20 AMERICAN FLAT |
| 9 MULETOWN | 21 LOWER RANCHERIA |
| 10 LIVE OAK | 22 SUMMIT CITY |
| 11 CARBONDALE | 23 FOREST HOME |
| 12 RANLETT | 24 FORT JOHN |

| | |
|---|---|
| 25 MISERY FLAT | 37 CONTRERAS |
| 26 ENTERPRISE | 38 SLABTOWN |
| 27 SPANISH GULCH | 39 POKERVILLE |
| 28 AQUEDUCT | 40 JACALITO |
| 29 JACKASS GULCH | 41 CHAPARRAL HILL |
| 30 SANTA MARIA GULCH | 42 WINTERS BAR |
| 31 COLUMBIA BAR | 43 POVERTY BAR |
| 32 CHIMA GULCH | 44 COPPER CENTER |
| 33 UNION BAR | 45 BLOOD GULCH |
| 34 PUT'S BAR | 46 YEOMET |
| 35 FORT ANN | 47 BUTTON WILLOW |
| 36 ARKANSAS FERRY | 48 QUIEN SABE? |

The hills are not called golden merely because gold lies hidden beneath them. The ever-changing seasons produce an array of gold in splendid abundance, each in its own time. Springtime brings hillsides covered with the golden poppy . . . summer brings the gold of dried grasses against an azure sky . . . autumn turns the leaves of the oak, the cottonwood, the dogwood and the quaking aspen into pillars of bright yellow-gold. There is no more beautiful land on the face of the earth. We hope this book will help you enjoy it and that you will treasure the many golden memories of your travels in the Golden Hills.

# Appendix

## For Further Information

The following is a list of organizations which can assist you in planning your vacation:

FOREST SUPERVISOR, Sierra National Forest
Federal Building, Room 3017
1130 "O" Street, Fresno, California 93721
(209) 487-5155

LAKE DON PEDRO MARINA
81 Bonds Flat Road
La Grange, California 95329

FOREST SUPERVISOR, El Dorado National Forest
100 Forni Road
Placerville, California 95667

CAMANCHE LAKE PARK
P.O. Box 92, Wallace, California 95254
(209) 763-5178

MARIPOSA CHAMBER OF COMMERCE
Mariposa, California 95338

NEW HOGAN LAKE
(209) 772-1343

CHAW-SE and COLUMBIA State Historical Parks
Department of Parks and Recreation
P.O. Box 2390, Sacramento, California 95811

CALAVERAS COUNTY CHAMBER OF COMMERCE
P.O. Box 177, San Andreas, California 95249
(209) 754-3391

BEAR VALLEY MARKETING ASSOCIATION
Bear Valley, California 95223

ARTA (American River Touring Association)
1016 Jackson Street, Oakland, California 94607
(415) 465-9355

TUOLUMNE COUNTY CHAMBER OF COMMERCE
P.O. Box 277, Sonora, California 95370

CALAVERAS BIG TREES STATE PARK
P.O. Box 686, Arnold, California 95223
(209) 795-1181

CLAYPIPERS THEATER, Drytown
For reservations call (415) 593-2742

BEAN HOLLOW HUNTING PRESERVE
(Camanche North Shore)
(209) 763-5144

GOOSE HILL GUN CLUB
Ione, California 95640
(209) 274-2175

ZEPHYR RIVER EXPEDITIONS
P.O. Box 529, Columbia, California 95310
(209) 532-6249

PINECREST LAKE RESORT
P.O. Box 1216, Pinecrest, California 95364
(209) 965-3411

JUMPING FROG JUBILEE
P.O. Box 96, Angels Camp, California 95222

AMADOR COUNTY CHAMBER OF COMMERCE
P.O. Box 596, Jackson, California 95642
(209) 223-0350

The following books are recommended for further reading:

*Amador County History*, Reprint of 1927 publication, Amador Publishing Co., Jackson, 1977.

*The Annals of Mokelumne Hill, The Story of a Veritable Gold Mountain*, compiled by Emmett P. Joy, published by the Old Timers Museum, Murphys, 1975.

*Annals of Tuolumne County*, by Thomas R. Stoddart, Valley Publishers, Fresno, 1977.

*The Big Oak Flat Road to Yosemite*, by Irene Poden and Margaret Schlichtmann, Holmes Book Co., Oakland, 1959.

*Big Tree - Carson Valley Turnpike, Ebbetts Pass and Highway Four*, by R. Coke Wood, published by the Old Timers Museum, Murphys, 1968.

*The Call of Gold*, by Newell D. Chamberlain, Valley Publishers, Fresno, 1977.

*Ghost Towns of Amador County*, by John Andrews, Valley Publishers, Fresno, 1978.

*Joaquin Murrieta*, by Yellow Bird (John Rollin Ridge), University of Oklahoma Press, Norman, Oklahoma, 1955.

*Short Line to Paradise, The Story of the Yosemite Valley Railroad*, by Hank Johnston, Flying Spur Press, Yosemite, 1962.

*Tales of California*, by Russell C. Grigsby, Mother Lode Press, Sonora, 1966.

*Miwok Means People*, by Eugene L. Conrotto, Valley Publishers, Fresno, 1973.

# Index